Six Poets

Six Poets

Hardy to Larkin

An anthology by

ALAN BENNETT

FABER & FABER

P

PROFILE BOOKS

First published in 1990
as *Poetry in Motion*
by Channel 4 Television
60 Charlotte Street, London W1P 2AX

This edition first published in 2014
by Faber & Faber Ltd
Bloomsbury House, 74–77 Great Russell Street
London WC1B 3DA
www.faber.co.uk

and

Profile Books Ltd
3a Exmouth House
Pine Street, Exmouth Market
London EC1R 0JH
www.profilebooks.com

Typeset by Country Setting, Kingsdown, Kent CT14 8ES

Printed in England by CPI Group (UK) Ltd, Croydon, CR0 4YY

Editorial material © Alan Bennett, 1990, 2014

Poems © the Estates of the individual authors

The right of Alan Bennett to be identified as author
of this work has been asserted in accordance with Section 77
of the Copyright, Designs and Patents Act 1988

A CIP record for this book
is available from the British Library

ISBN 978–0–571–32109–4
EBOOK ISBN 978–0–571–32184–1

Contents

Introduction

When I was young, I used to feel that literature was a club of which I would never be a proper member as a reader, let alone a writer. It wasn't that I didn't read books, or even the 'right' books, but I always felt that the ones I read couldn't be literature if only because I had read them. It was the books I couldn't get into (and these included most poetry) that constituted literature – or, rather, Literature.

After a lifetime, these feelings of impotence and exclusion are still fresh in my mind. I have only to hear someone extolling the charms of Byron, say, or Coleridge, neither of whom I've ever managed to read, to be reminded of how baffled one can feel in the face of books.

Mindful of this, when I put together *Poetry in Motion*, the Channel 4 series from which this book derives, I didn't make any bones about admitting what I didn't understand or sympathise with. I'm all at sea with much of Auden, for instance, but feel less of a fool saying so because that kind of plain speaking is a refreshing feature of Auden's own literary criticism. Auden is an exception, though, because the poets and poems I chose are all in differing degrees accessible. This seemed to me essential. Obviously, any poem repays study, but if it is only to be heard once and without detailed exposition, then a poem should be understandable at first hearing.

'Accessible' is another way of saying 'popular', and at least three of these poets – Housman, Betjeman and Larkin – are popular poets, much read and often quoted. The more a poet is read, the less he is written about. Criticism prefers an enigma, so Auden's opaque and highly allusive verse has received much more critical attention than that of Betjeman or Housman, though since the enigma of Housman lies more in his life than in his art, he has had more than his share of biography.

That clarity should be penalised by critical neglect is perhaps unfair, though it's not every writer who welcomes critical attention. 'I am more or less happy when being praised,' wrote the politician Arthur Balfour, 'not very comfortable when being abused, but I have moments of uneasiness when being explained.' While Balfour was not a poet, few writers enjoy being grilled about their text, hoping that they've made themselves clear, and if they haven't, that's a way of saying something, too. Posthumous commentary they can't do much about, but famished for subjects, some critics don't wait for death before hacking a chunk off their chosen prey and retiring to the academic undergrowth to chew it over. Auden suffered this fate, though airily. Larkin escaped it, perhaps because he had made his distaste so plain. In his poem 'Posterity', for instance, he imagines Jake Balokowsky, his fictional biographer, musing over the character of his subject: '"What's he like? . . . One of those old-type *natural* fouled-up guys."' But if, while he lived, Larkin kept the commentators at bay, his death in 1985 gave criticism the green light, and the hearse was followed by a volume of critical essays, many of them couched in terms that would have made the poet groan.

It was Larkin, though, who said that a crude difference between novels and poetry is that novels are about other people and poetry is about yourself. This isn't beyond dispute – Hardy, for instance, discouraged the reading of his poems as personal documents – but there is enough truth in it to justify an approach to these six poets through their lives. Justify it in Britain, that is – the current taste for biography (and gossip) about literary figures being a peculiarity of the English-speaking. It mystifies the Germans and the French, and it irritates authors, too. Hardy put together an official version of his life, which he fathered on the second Mrs Hardy, hoping that it would put paid to further revelations. Auden insisted (while enjoying biography himself) that his own biography should not be written – a useless embargo as since his death there have been any number – and while Larkin did not expressly forbid a biography, the bonfires burned in his garden just as they had in Hardy's.

A writer's motives in wanting an authorised version (or no version at all) of his or her life vary. Everybody has something to hide (even if it's only that they have nothing to hide), but writers in particular feel that, since they have erected a monument in the shape of their work, a second (or a third or a fourth) tombstone is neither necessary nor desirable. They could point to Kafka, who has practically got a cemetery to himself.

Readers for their part tend to imagine that the poem is just what the poet has seen fit to put in the shop window and that there's something tastier under the counter, which it is the job of the biographer to sniff out. Whether this turns out to be the case or not, writers ought to realise that any attempt to supervise their posthumous reputation is futile (though a surviving spouse tethered to the grave works wonders in scaring off trespassers). And some knowledge of a poet's life must add to the pleasure and understanding of his or her poetry. What the poet is afraid of is that the life will somehow invalidate the art (cries of 'He's insincere!', 'She's inconsistent!'). But you can enjoy literary biography while at the same time recognising that the literary works, once written, have an independent existence, regardless of the circumstances in which they were produced. Hardy's poems lyrically recalling Emma, his first wife, are not diminished as poems because of the truth (or the other truth) that the poet had treated Emma pretty shabbily. Though one could excuse the estate agent who, having read Auden's 'In Praise of Limestone', sends the poet a prospectus of desirable residences set amid the chuckling springs of rural Westmorland, only to be told that what the perfidious bastard really prefers is a shack on the parched island of Ischia.

Certain authors have fan clubs: Jane Austen, Anthony Trollope, Lewis Carroll and, more recently, Anthony Powell. Their work gets fenced off by enthusiasts, and the casual reader may feel the need of credentials to read them. Poets don't have fans in quite this way, though in the days of 'the love that dare not speak its name' Housman was a telltale volume to have on the bookshelf, along with Forrest Reid, say, or Denton Welch. And Betjeman began as a somewhat eccentric taste, his admirers a bit of a club, before the poetry made a space for itself and was taken up by the nation.

One link between these six poets is that all of them (with the possible exception of Hardy) admired Hardy. Auden explains why:

> My first Master was Thomas Hardy, and I think I was very lucky in my choice. He was a good poet, perhaps a great one, but not too good. Much as I loved him, even I could see his diction was often clumsy and forced and that a lot of his poems were plain bad. This gave me hope where a flawless poet might have made me despair.

Auden in his turn was admired by Larkin and MacNeice, though they were just two among the many poets he influenced. Auden was a good poet and perhaps a great one, though far from flawless, but he is less help to someone starting out than Hardy. Auden's tone of voice is distinctive and easy to imitate, and even when his poems are bad, they are couched in his peculiar imagery, and that is infectious, too. Half the job of learning to write is getting to know the sound of your own voice, and Auden is no help here at all, just spawning imitators.

Auden's intellect was formidable and showy, and quite off-putting. As an undergraduate at Oxford in 1956, I happened to hear his inaugural lecture as Professor of Poetry. I say 'happened to hear' because I didn't honestly have much interest in his poetry, knowing only that this was a fabled figure and wanting to take a look. Had I any ambitions to write at that time, the lecture would have been enough to put me off. Auden listed all the interests and accomplishments that poets and critics should properly have – a dream of Eden, an ideal landscape, favourite books, even, God help us, a passion for Icelandic sagas. If writing means passing this kind of kit inspection, I thought, one might as well forget it.

MacNeice would probably have been more encouraging. He's the odd man out among these six poets. Never well known enough to be other than a private face, MacNeice did not have to deal with the consequences of reputation, did not have to imitate himself, for instance, or sidestep his fame as his better-known colleagues had to learn to do. It might have happened, but because he died relatively young, he was denied his proper place. I didn't know his poetry and to discover it was one of the pleasures of putting together this anthology.

I would like to acknowledge the help of Channel 4, for which the original *Poetry in Motion* programmes were made. They were conceived and filmed by Tony Cash, whom I have known practically all my life, even briefly sharing a desk with him in the sixth form at Leeds Modern School in the 1950s. He has been a constant encouragement, as has my editor Dinah Wood.

Six Poets

Thomas Hardy

1840–1928

Despite humble origins – his mother was a cook, his father a fiddle-playing stonemason – Thomas Hardy achieved such fame that he was awarded the Order of Merit and his ashes now lie in Westminster Abbey. Most of his life was spent in Dorset, the county of his birth. Aged sixteen he trained then practised as an architect. Success came in 1880 with the novel *The Trumpet-Major: A Tale*, published in instalments, as were *Tess of the D'Urbervilles*, *The Mayor of Casterbridge* and his last major work of fiction, *Jude the Obscure*, serialised in 1894–5. From 1898 until his death, he committed himself to poetry, finding inspiration in ancient and medieval history as well as the Napoleonic Wars: he even interviewed veterans of the Napoleonic campaigns and visited the battle-field of Waterloo. The last thirty years were largely spent at Max Gate, a house he himself designed near Dorchester. He lived there with his first wife, Emma Gifford, and, after she died in 1912, with his second wife, Florence Dugdale, a school-teacher and writer of children's stories. The pall bearers at his funeral included A. E. Housman, Rudyard Kipling and George Bernard Shaw. Spared cremation, his heart was buried in Emma's grave in the churchyard at Stinsford in Dorset, within walking distance of his birthplace.

Beeny Cliff

March 1870–March 1913

I

O the opal and the sapphire of that wandering western sea,
And the woman riding high above with bright hair flapping free –
The woman whom I loved so, and who loyally loved me.

II

The pale mews plained below us, and the waves seemed far away
In a nether sky, engrossed in saying their ceaseless babbling say,
As we laughed light-heartedly aloft on that clear-sunned March day.

III

A little cloud then cloaked us, and there flew an irised rain,
And the Atlantic dyed its levels with a dull misfeatured stain,
And then the sun burst out again, and purples prinked the main.

IV

– Still in all its chasmal beauty bulks old Beeny to the sky,
And shall she and I not go there once again now March is nigh,
And the sweet things said in that March say anew there by and by?

V

What if still in chasmal beauty looms that wild weird western shore,
The woman now is – elsewhere – whom the ambling pony bore,
And nor knows nor cares for Beeny, and will laugh there nevermore.

Hardy was seventy-two when he wrote that poem, and he was remembering a visit to Cornwall some forty years earlier, when he met Emma Gifford, whom he later married. She had died a few months before he wrote 'Beeny Cliff', which was part of a flood of verse released by her death. It wasn't so much grief as remorse: Hardy and his wife hadn't got on. She was vague, fey and, some people said, mad. It's a thankless role, being an artist's wife. Writers want a wife, but they also want a disciple, someone who can do the buttering-up as well as the washing-up. Emma Hardy wasn't really suited to either because she had literary ambitions of her own, so Hardy had to look elsewhere for appreciation.

He found it in various grand ladies, enamoured of litera-ture and untrammelled by Emma's domestic duties. One of them was his secretary Florence Dugdale, who after a decent interval became the second Mrs Hardy. This wasn't a great success either, because Hardy spent most of this marriage, as can be seen in the poem, recalling the supposed delights of his first. So the first Mrs Hardy had the last laugh. It's the kind of story Hardy could have written – life, as so often, imitating art.

The second Mrs Hardy might have known what was coming from the manner of Hardy's proposal. He had taken her to the churchyard to show her the grave of Wife No. 1, and, pointing to another vacant plot, he said, 'That's for you.' By this, she took it that he was proposing. Before they're anything else, if they're any good at all, most writers are absurd.

Graves, though, had a fascination for Hardy. This is a poem about a yew tree in a churchyard:

Transformations

Portion of this yew
Is a man my grandsire knew,
Bosomed here at its foot:
This branch may be his wife,
A ruddy human life
Now turned to a green shoot.

These grasses must be made
Of her who often prayed,
Last century, for repose;
And the fair girl long ago
Whom I often tried to know
May be entering this rose.

So, they are not underground,
But as nerves and veins abound
In the growths of upper air,
And they feel the sun and rain,
And the energy again
That made them what they were!

Hardy was at home in churches. He knew the morning and evening services by heart, and though he had lost his faith as a young man, he continued to go to church and indeed designed one at Turnworth near his home at Max Gate in Dorset. He sometimes used to cycle there to read the lesson at morning service. It was a ride of twenty-odd miles, and as Hardy stood at the lectern, the congregation would see his bald head steaming gently.

In Church

'And now to God the Father,' he ends,
And his voice thrills up to the topmost tiles:
Each listener chokes as he bows and bends,
And emotion pervades the crowded aisles.
Then the preacher glides to the vestry-door,
And shuts it, and thinks he is seen no more.

The door swings softly ajar meanwhile,
And a pupil of his in the Bible class,
Who adores him as one without gloss or guile,
Sees her idol stand with a satisfied smile
And re-enact at the vestry-glass
Each pulpit gesture in deft dumb-show
That had moved the congregation so.

That's very much a novelist's poem, an incident, no moral drawn, just his vanity, her disillusion, the way things are, the poet simply putting a frame round it. Hardy's poems seldom offer consolation even when that consolation might just amount to some hint of meaning or sense in the universe. Religion certainly had none for Hardy; when he was eighty-nine, he scribbled down a bitter verse called 'Christmas: 1924'.

Christmas: 1924

'Peace upon earth!' was said. We sing it,
And pay a million priests to bring it.
After two thousand years of mass
We've got as far as poison-gas.

Hardy had given up writing novels in 1896 after the hostile reception of *Jude the Obscure*, a copy of which, it's particularly worth noting today, was burned publicly by a bishop. He had written poetry all his life and now devoted himself exclusively to it. I suspect that it was what Virginia Woolf called the 'architecting' of novels that no longer appealed to him. Poetry has it over the novel in that it uses fewer words. You can do more with less.

He did, though, write one huge poem – *The Dynasts*, about the Napoleonic wars. Some of it is windy and sprawling, but Hardy was nothing if not down to earth (it's part of his fascination with graves). Here is a section about the night before Waterloo, but not about the common soldiers as Shakespeare might have done it, but the common creatures, disturbed by the preparations for the coming battle.

The Eve of Waterloo

(*from* The Dynasts)

The eyelids of eve fall together at last,
And the forms so foreign to field and tree
Lie down as though native, and slumber fast!

Sore are the thrills of misgiving we see
In the artless champaign at this harlequinade,
Distracting a vigil where calm should be!

The green seems opprest, and the Plain afraid
Of a Something to come, whereof these are the proofs –
Neither earthquake, nor storm, nor eclipse's shade!

Yea, the coneys are scared by the thud of hoofs,
And their white scuts flash at their vanishing heels,
And swallows abandon the hamlet-roofs.

The mole's tunnelled chambers are crushed by wheels,
The lark's eggs are scattered, their owners fled;
And the hedgehog's household the sapper unseals.

The snail draws in at the terrible tread,
But in vain; he is crushed by the felloe-rim;
The worm asks what can be overheard,

And wriggles deep from a scene so grim,
And guesses him safe; for he does not know
What a foul red flood will be soaking him!

Beaten about by the heel and toe
Are butterflies, sick of the day's long rheum,
To die of a worse than the weather-foe.

Trodden and bruised to a miry tomb
Are ears that have greened but will never be gold,
And flowers in the bud that will never bloom.

So the season's intent, ere its fruit unfold,
Is frustrate, and mangled, and made succumb,
Like a youth of promise struck stark and cold! . . .

———————————————

Some of that sympathy with the unredeemed lives of small creatures found its way into many of Hardy's poems. Once, when he was a boy in Dorset, he was crossing the field where the sheep were penned and took it into his head to get down on his hands and knees and pretend to crop the grass to see what it was like to be a sheep. When he looked up, the whole flock was gathered round him, gazing at him with astonished faces.

The railway hadn't reached Dorset when Hardy was born in 1840, but when it did, it was, of course, the Great Western, with its terminus at Paddington. It has been said that in London you settle near the station you arrive at, and when Hardy came to London to work as an architect, he lived in Bayswater and was married at St Peter's, Paddington. Several of his poems are set on the railway, including this:

At the Railway Station, Upway

'There is not much that I can do,
  For I've no money that's quite my own!'
  Spoke up the pitying child –
A little boy with a violin
At the station before the train came in, –
'But I can play my fiddle to you,
And a nice one 'tis, and good in tone!'

  The man in the handcuffs smiled;
The constable looked, and he smiled, too,
  As the fiddle began to twang;
And the man in the handcuffs suddenly sang
        With grimful glee:
        'This life so free
        Is the thing for me!'
And the constable smiled, and said no word,
As if unconscious of what he heard;
And so they went on till the train came in –
The convict, and boy with the violin.

Another of Hardy's poems set on a train is a poetic version of a scene that occurs with much the same details in his last novel, *Jude the Obscure*.

Midnight on the Great Western

In the third-class seat sat the journeying boy,
    And the roof-lamp's oily flame
Played down on his listless form and face,
Bewrapt past knowing to what he was going,
    Or whence he came.

In the band of his hat the journeying boy
    Had a ticket stuck; and a string
Around his neck bore the key of his box,
That twinkled gleams of the lamp's sad beams
    Like a living thing.

What past can be yours, O journeying boy
    Towards a world unknown,
Who calmly, as if incurious quite
On all at stake, can undertake
    This plunge alone?

Knows your soul a sphere, O journeying boy,
    Our rude realms far above,
Whence with spacious vision you mark and mete
This region of sin that you find you in,
    But are not of?

Hardy was the son of a jobbing builder, but many of his relations were farm labourers and some had been born in the workhouse. At Hardy's funeral service in Westminster Abbey, an old tramp had somehow got himself into the reserved seats. A clergyman neighbour of the Hardys got into conversation with him, thinking he'd just come in from the cold, but he found to his surprise that the tramp knew a great deal about Hardy and indeed was probably one of his relatives.

Quite early in his life, Hardy began to cut himself off socially from his lowly background, while artistically he drew on it more and more. He even tried to bump up his social origins, making a great deal of even the vaguest of well-to-do connections (exactly the opposite of what a writer would do today). When he was an old man and a celebrity, he was visited by the Prince of Wales (later the Duke of Windsor), to whom he gave lunch. The gardener, who was as much a social climber as Hardy, but on a lower slope, appropriated the chicken bone that the Prince had gnawed, as a souvenir.

Hardy's poems are sometimes like entries in a writer's (or a film-maker's) notebook. Complete in itself, this poem is also a note for a scene that could become a longer story.

The Whitewashed Wall

Why does she turn in that shy soft way
    Whenever she stirs the fire,
And kiss to the chimney-corner wall,
    As if entranced to admire
Its whitewashed bareness more than the sight
    Of a rose in richest green?
I have known her long, but this raptured rite
    I never before have seen.

– Well, once when her son cast his shadow there,
    A friend took a pencil and drew him
Upon that flame-lit wall. And the lines
    Had a lifelike semblance to him.
And there long stayed his familiar look;
    But one day, ere she knew,
The whitener came to cleanse the nook,
    And covered the face from view.

'Yes,' he said: 'My brush goes on with a rush,
    And the draught is buried under;
When you have to whiten old cots and brighten,
    What else can you do, I wonder?'
But she knows he's there. And when she yearns
    For him, deep in the labouring night,
She sees him as close at hand, and turns
    To him under his sheet of white.

Hardy's verse is often a bit ungainly; it doesn't always run smooth. One of the reasons for this is that he melds ordinary conversation with the verse, and even, as in this next poem, bits of advertising copy. It's this casual style that has made him a greater influence on later poets than, say, Eliot or Yeats, who have had more acclaim. Auden, Betjeman and Larkin – all owe a good deal to Hardy.

At the Draper's

'I stood at the back of the shop, my dear,
    But you did not perceive me.
Well, when they deliver what you were shown
    I shall know nothing of it, believe me!'

And he coughed and coughed as she paled and said,
    'O, I didn't see you come in there –
Why couldn't you speak?' – 'Well, I didn't. I left
    That you should not notice I'd been there.

'You were viewing some lovely things. *"Soon required
    For a widow, of latest fashion"*;
And I knew 'twould upset you to meet the man
    Who had to be cold and ashen

'And screwed in a box before they could dress you
    "In the last new note in mourning",
As they defined it. So, not to distress you,
    I left you to your adorning.'

Now a happier poem, though like so many of Hardy's, it ends with a grave. It's a poem to his cat. Samuel Butler said that the true test of the imagination is the ability to name a cat, but T. S. Eliot said that cats have several names, including the name they're given and the name that they eventually acquire. The name that Hardy's cat eventually acquired was Kiddleywinkempoops Trot.

Last Words to a Dumb Friend

Pet was never mourned as you,
Purrer of the spotless hue,
Plumy tail, and wistful gaze
While you humoured our queer ways,
Or outshrilled your morning call
Up the stairs and through the hall –
Foot suspended in its fall –
While, expectant, you would stand
Arched, to meet the stroking hand;
Till your way you chose to wend
Yonder, to your tragic end.

Never another pet for me!
Let your place all vacant be;
Better blankness day by day
Than companion torn away.
Better bid his memory fade,
Better blot each mark he made,
Selfishly escape distress
By contrived forgetfulness,
Than preserve his prints to make
Every morn and eve an ache.

From the chair whereon he sat
Sweep his fur, nor wince thereat;
Rake his little pathways out
Mid the bushes roundabout;
Smooth away his talons' mark
From the claw-worn pine-tree bark,
Where he climbed as dusk embrowned,
Waiting us who loitered round.

Strange it is this speechless thing,
Subject to our mastering,
Subject for his life and food
To our gift, and time, and mood;
Timid pensioner of us Powers,
His existence ruled by ours,
Should – by crossing at a breath
Into safe and shielded death,
By the merely taking hence
Of his insignificance –
Loom as largened to the sense,
Shape as part, above man's will,
Of the Imperturbable.

As a prisoner, flight debarred,
Exercising in a yard,
Still retain I, troubled, shaken,
Mean estate, by him forsaken;
And this home, which scarcely took
Impress from his little look,
By his faring to the Dim
Grows all eloquent of him.

Housemate, I can think you still
Bounding to the window-sill,
Over which I vaguely see
Your small mound beneath the tree,
Showing in the autumn shade
That you moulder where you played.

2 October 1904

———————

Hardy never said much about writing or the difficulties of it, or the moral difficulties of it. Kafka said that a writer was doing the devil's work, writing a wholly inadequate response to the brutishness of the world, and Hardy increasingly felt this. It's not that it's an immoral activity or an amoral one; it's just that the act of creation is something to which the ordinary standards of human behaviour do not apply.

Hardy never liked to be touched. He always walked in the road to avoid brushing against people, and servants were told never to help him on with his coat and just to drop the shawl around his shoulders and not tuck him in. The pen had been his weapon in his struggle for life – and it had been a struggle.

The next poem is a dialogue with the moon.

I Looked Up from My Writing

I looked up from my writing,
    And gave a start to see,
As if rapt in my inditing,
    The moon's full gaze on me.

Her meditative misty head
    Was spectral in its air,
And I involuntarily said,
    'What are you doing there?'

'Oh, I've been scanning pond and hole
    And waterway hereabout
For the body of one with a sunken soul
    Who has put his life-light out.

'Did you hear his frenzied tattle?
    It was sorrow for his son
Who is slain in brutish battle,
    Though he has injured none.

'And now I am curious to look
    Into the blinkered mind
Of one who wants to write a book
    In a world of such a kind.'

Her temper overwrought me,
    And I edged to shun her view,
For I felt assured she thought me
    One who should drown him too.

Now one of Hardy's greatest poems.

The Convergence of the Twain

(Lines on the loss of the Titanic)

I

In a solitude of the sea
Deep from human vanity,
And the Pride of Life that planned her, stilly couches she.

II

Steel chambers, late the pyres
Of her salamandrine fires,
Cold currents thrid, and turn to rhythmic tidal lyres.

III

Over the mirrors meant
To glass the opulent
The sea-worm crawls – grotesque, slimed, dumb, indifferent.

IV

Jewels in joy designed
To ravish the sensuous mind
Lie lightless, all their sparkles bleared and black and blind.

V

Dim moon-eyed fishes near
Gaze at the gilded gear
And query: 'What does this vaingloriousness down here?'

VI

Well: while was fashioning
This creature of cleaving wing,
The Immanent Will that stirs and urges everything

VII

Prepared a sinister mate
For her – so gaily great –
A Shape of Ice, for the time far and dissociate.

VIII

And as the smart ship grew
In stature, grace, and hue,
In shadowy silent distance grew the Iceberg too.

IX

Alien they seemed to be:
No mortal eye could see
The intimate welding of their later history,

X

Or sign that they were bent
By paths coincident
On being anon twin halves of one august event,

XI

Till the Spinner of the Years
Said 'Now!' And each one hears,
The consummation comes, and jars two hemispheres.

———————————

Hardy died in 1928. His life had spanned a great length of time. One hot, humid day when he was a child, his grandmother had said to him, 'It was like this in the French Revolution, I remember.' When he was born in 1840, the railway had not reached Dorset; when he died, the news went by telephone to London and was immediately broadcast by the BBC.

Although his ashes were buried in Westminster Abbey, his relatives who thought they knew him better, knew he was at heart a peasant like they were, claimed his heart for their own, and that was buried in Dorset. 'Ache deep,' Hardy had written,

> . . . but make no moans:
> Smile not; but stilly suffer:
> The paths of love are rougher
> Than thoroughfares of stones.

And when he lay on his deathbed, his sister noted on his face 'the same triumphant look that all the others bore . . . but without the smile'.

Two poems to end with. First, a poem of the Boer War:

Drummer Hodge

I

They throw in Drummer Hodge, to rest
    Uncoffined – just as found:
His landmark is a kopje-crest
    That breaks the veldt around;
And foreign constellations west
    Each night above his mound.

II

Young Hodge the Drummer never knew –
    Fresh from his Wessex home –
The meaning of the broad Karoo,
    The Bush, the dusty loam,
And why uprose to nightly view
    Strange stars amid the gloam.

III

Yet portion of that unknown plain
    Will Hodge for ever be;
His homely Northern breast and brain
    Grow to some Southern tree,
And strange-eyed constellations reign
    His stars eternally.

That poem – the young soldier killed far from home and his grave watched over by alien stars – calls to mind the poet whom I shall be turning to next, A. E. Housman. But I'll end with a little nature poem and one that is, for Hardy, almost cheerful.

Proud Songsters

The thrushes sing as the sun is going,
And the finches whistle in ones and pairs,
And as it gets dark loud nightingales
     In bushes,
Pipe, as they can when April wears,
       As if all Time were theirs.

These are brand-new birds of twelve-months' growing,
Which a year ago, or less than twain,
No finches were, nor nightingales,
     Nor thrushes,
But only particles of grain,
       And earth, and air, and rain.

A. E. Housman

1859–1936

Alfred Edward Housman, son of a solicitor and eldest of seven siblings, was born in Fockbury, Worcestershire, and educated at St John's College, Oxford. Failing his finals, he found work as a clerk in the London Patent Office but continued to study the classics, publishing articles when he could. In 1892, ten years after leaving Oxford, he was appointed Professor of Latin at University College London and, in 1911, at Cambridge. His first poetry collection, *A Shropshire Lad*, was published in 1896, followed by *Last Poems* in 1922 and *More Poems* in 1936. His principal scholarly concern was to ensure the authenticity of old texts, and he has been highly praised by classicists for his editions of Roman poets including Juvenal, Lucan and Manilius. After his death and burial in Ludlow, Shropshire, many composers – among them Ralph Vaughan Williams, Ivor Gurney, George Butterworth and the American Samuel Barber – set his poems to music.

On Wenlock Edge

(*from* A Shropshire Lad)

On Wenlock Edge the wood's in trouble;
 His forest fleece the Wrekin heaves;
The gale, it plies the saplings double,
 And thick on Severn snow the leaves.

'Twould blow like this through holt and hanger
 When Uricon the city stood:
'Tis the old wind in the old anger,
 But then it threshed another wood.

Then, 'twas before my time, the Roman
 At yonder heaving hill would stare:
The blood that warms an English yeoman,
 The thoughts that hurt him, they were there.

There, like the wind through woods in riot,
 Through him the gale of life blew high;
The tree of man was never quiet:
 Then 'twas the Roman, now 'tis I.

The gale, it plies the saplings double,
 It blows so hard, 'twill soon be gone:
To-day the Roman and his trouble
 Are ashes under Uricon.

My dear sir,

You seem to admire my poems even more than I admire them myself, which is very noble of you, but will most likely be difficult to keep up for any great length of time.

As to your queries: I wrote the book, *A Shropshire Lad*, when I was thirty-five and I expect to write another when I am seventy, by which time your enthusiasm will have had time to cool. My trade is that of Professor of Latin in this college: I suppose that my classical training has been of some use to me in furnishing good models, and making me fastidious, and telling me what to leave out. My chief object in publishing my verses was to give pleasure to a few young men here and there, and I am glad if they have given pleasure to you.

I am yours very truly,

A. E. HOUSMAN

Housman had been brought up and educated as a child in Worcestershire, and his poems are set in the counties of his boyhood: Worcestershire, Shropshire and the Welsh Marches. He practised what – in the above letter, written to the American poet Witter Bynner in June 1903 – he called his 'trade' as professor of Latin at University College London, and in 1911 he moved to Cambridge, so apart from a period as a civil servant when he was a young man, he was a don and a professor all his adult life. He was also a poet all his life, insofar as, long before he published any poetry, he was keeping notebooks. His output didn't follow quite the restricted pattern his letter suggests, but he was never prolific, most of his energies going into his academic work. In this he was pre-eminent, one of the foremost scholars of his time, whose range and scholarship were so formidable he might just as easily have become a professor of Greek as a professor of Latin.

Housman was not an easy man. Timid in appearance – someone said of him that he looked as if he came from a long line of maiden aunts – he could be caustic and severe, and was ruthless with intellects less gifted than his own and with any form of slipshod work. 'The faintest of all human passions', he said, 'is the love of truth,' but not with him, and from that love of truth came a mistrust of religion as profound as that of Hardy. But he was shy and austere. Virginia Woolf used to talk of T. S. Eliot and his four-piece suits, and though Housman's poetry is nothing if not confessional, he was even more buttoned up than Eliot, whose 'I grow old . . . I grow old . . . I shall wear the bottoms of my trousers rolled' has an echo in Housman.

From the Wash

(*from* More Poems)

From the wash the laundress sends
My collars home with ravelled ends:
I must fit, now these are frayed,
My neck with new ones London-made.

Homespun collars, homespun hearts,
Wear to rags in foreign parts.
Mine at least's as good as done,
And I must get a London one.

One gets from the poems – and if one were to select them almost at random, it would be the same – the notes Housman sounds again and again in his verse, his tonic sol-fa: youth, a glory that cannot last, a sunset light and death that is just over the horizon, with only the best dying young. The thought is classical, but, in the way Housman hitches death to war or to the gallows or to suicide, it is a romantic vision, and over it all there is the sense of lost love. And the other element that one picks up as these soldiers go off to war, or to some other distant dying, is that the poet is a bystander. He has no part in these deaths, or if he does, it is because he has no part in these lives.

To an Athlete Dying Young

(*from* A Shropshire Lad)

The time you won your town the race
We chaired you through the market-place;
Man and boy stood cheering by,
And home we brought you shoulder-high.

Today, the road all runners come,
Shoulder-high we bring you home,
And set you at your threshold down,
Townsman of a stiller town.

Smart lad, to slip betimes away
From fields where glory does not stay
And early though the laurel grows
It withers quicker than the rose.

Eyes the shady night has shut
Cannot see the record cut,
And silence sounds no worse than cheers
After earth has stopped the ears:

Now you will not swell the rout
Of lads that wore their honours out,
Runners whom renown outran
And the name died before the man.

So set, before its echoes fade,
The fleet foot on the sill of shade,
And hold to the low lintel up
The still-defended challenge-cup.

And round that early-laurelled head
Will flock to gaze the strengthless dead,
And find unwithered on its curls
The garland briefer than a girl's.

Housman's first book of poems from which that poem was taken was called *A Shropshire Lad*, but he had no rural connections and didn't even know Shropshire very well. The son of a Worcestershire solicitor, he went to Bromsgrove School, then to Oxford, lived for a while in London and spent the rest of his life in Cambridge. So the personnel of his poetry was invented and the landscape a setting.

What was at the heart of his writing, at any rate to begin with, was an unrequited passion for a fellow Oxford undergraduate, Moses Jackson – a thoroughly straightforward, unreflective young man who, if he was ever aware of Housman's affection, chose that it should never be made specific. In a less single-minded character than Housman's, such a passion might have been expected to pass and be replaced by other, perhaps happier, affections. And insofar as Housman became friendly with Jackson's younger brother, it may have done so. But the brother died and Housman was left with these affections, and the memory of them, all his life. Jackson went off to India, became principal of a teacher training college there and then took a similar post in Canada. *A Shropshire Lad* is dedicated to him, but when asked what had caused him to write the poems, Housman said it was a period of mild ill-health – a prolonged sore throat.

Shake Hands

(*from* More Poems)

Shake hands, we shall never be friends, all's over;
   I only vex you the more I try.
All's wrong that ever I've done or said,
And nought to help it in this dull head:
   Shake hands, here's luck, good-bye.

But if you come to a road where danger
   Or guilt or anguish or shame's to share,
Be good to the lad that loves you true
And the soul that was born to die for you,
   And whistle and I'll be there.

In the years that followed, the two friends met from time to time and Housman wrote regularly – but in the words of Auden's poem, 'Who's Who', Jackson 'answered some of his long, marvellous letters, but kept none'.

Because I liked you better

(*from* More Poems)

Because I liked you better
  Than suits a man to say,
It irked you, and I promised
  To throw the thought away.

To put the world between us
  We parted, stiff and dry;
'Good-bye,' said you, 'forget me.'
  'I will, no fear,' said I.

If here, where clover whitens
  The dead man's knoll, you pass,
And no tall flower to meet you
  Starts in the trefoiled grass,

Halt by the headstone naming
  The heart no longer stirred,
And say the lad that loved you
  Was one that kept his word.

Girls, it has to be said, only figure in Housman as an occasion for the deaths of boys. Their place in the scheme of things is to make lads unhappy so that they go off to war or hang themselves. This is sometimes quite difficult to take, and the word 'lads' is quite difficult to take now too, when its usage is largely confined to football managers: 'The lads played a blinder.' Jokes about Housman are easy to make, and with his simple forms and limited subject matter, his poetry has always been an easy target for parody, as in these verses by Hugh Kingsmill.

> What, still alive at twenty-two,
> A clean, upstanding chap like you?
> Sure, if your throat 'tis hard to slit,
> Slit your girl's, and swing for it.

> Like enough, you won't be glad,
> When they come to hang you, lad:
> But bacon's not the only thing
> That's cured by hanging from a string.

The next poem, a dialogue between a soldier and his sweet-heart, owes something to Hardy, whom Housman admired.

The Deserter

(*from* Last Poems)

'What sound awakened me, I wonder,
   For now 'tis dumb.'
'Wheels on the road most like, or thunder:
   Lie down; 'twas not the drum.'

Toil at sea and two in haven
   And trouble far:
Fly, crow, away, and follow, raven,
   And all that croaks for war.

'Hark, I heard the bugle crying,
   And where am I?
My friends are up and dressed and dying,
   And I will dress and die.'

'Oh love is rare and trouble plenty
   And carrion cheap,
And daylight dear at four-and-twenty:
   Lie down again and sleep.'

'Reach me my belt and leave your prattle:
   Your hour is gone;
But my day is the day of battle,
   And that comes dawning on.

'They mow the field of man in season:
    Farewell, my fair,
And, call it truth or call it treason,
    Farewell the vows that were.'

'Ay, false heart, forsake me lightly:
    'Tis like the brave.
They find no bed to joy in rightly
    Before they find the grave.

'Their love is for their own undoing,
    And east and west
They scour about the world a-wooing
    The bullet to their breast.

'Sail away the ocean over,
    Oh sail away,
And lie there with your leaden lover
    For ever and a day.'

———————————

Austere though Housman was, he could unbend with women and children, perhaps because, to him, they didn't really count. I'm not sure that his poems actually appeal to women; certainly I couldn't find any women critics who have written about them. When Housman was teaching at University College London his elaborate sarcasm would often reduce his women students to tears. Well, this they could just about take, but what really upset them was that, the following week, Housman could not remember which ones he had offended or even tell any of them apart.

A Shropshire Lad was written in 1894 and 1895. In the latter year, Housman wrote a much more explicit poem which was not included in the collection and was only published after his death. 1895 may have been the year of the publication of Housman's poems, but it was also the year of the trials of Oscar Wilde.

Oh Who is that Young Sinner

(*from* Additional Poems)

Oh who is that young sinner with the handcuffs on his wrists?
And what has he been after that they groan and shake their fists?
And wherefore is he wearing such a conscience-stricken air?
Oh they're taking him to prison for the colour of his hair.

'Tis a shame to human nature, such a head of hair as his;
In the good old time 'twas hanging for the colour that it is;
Though hanging isn't bad enough and flaying would be fair
For the nameless and abominable colour of his hair.

Oh a deal of pains he's taken and a pretty price he's paid
To hide his poll or dye it of a mentionable shade;
But they've pulled the beggar's hat off for all the world to see
    and stare,
And they're haling him to justice for the colour of his hair.

Now 'tis oakum for his fingers and the treadmill for his feet
And the quarry-gang on Portland in the cold and in the heat,
And between his spells of labour in the time he has to spare
He can curse the God that made him for the colour of his hair.

It's hard to imagine two writers more different than Housman and Wilde, but as one critic has said: 'From Wenlock Edge, one can see as far as Reading Gaol.' Housman saw it too and, after Wilde's release, he sent him a copy of *A Shropshire Lad*. He used to say with some pride that Robert Ross, Wilde's friend, had learned a few of the poems by heart and recited them to Wilde while he was still in gaol.

The occasion for Wilde's poem *The Ballad of Reading Gaol* was the hanging of a young soldier who had murdered his sweetheart, a situation Housman would have found familiar. Like Hardy, he was fascinated by hanging. As a boy, Hardy had seen a woman hanged and it haunted him all his life, and in Housman, too, the gallows are always turning up.

Eight O'Clock

(*from* Last Poems)

He stood and heard the steeple
   Sprinkle the quarters on the morning town.
One, two, three, four, to market-place and people
   It tossed them down.

Strapped, noosed, nighing his hour,
   He stood and counted them and cursed his luck;
And then the clock collected in the tower
   Its strength, and struck.

Another of Housman's gallows verses reads:

> But fetch the county kerchief
> And noose me in the knot,
> And I will rot.

The American lawyer Clarence Darrow amended the verse to make it read 'Fetch the county *sheriff* / And noose me in the knot' – and he got several murderers off by emotionally quoting the line to the jury. Housman said that it was partly due to him that Leopold and Loeb (who murdered a boy for kicks in the 1920s) escaped the gallows.

I did not lose my heart

(*from* More Poems)

I did not lose my heart in summer's even,
    When roses to the moonrise burst apart:
When plumes were under heel and lead was flying,
    In blood and smoke and flame I lost my heart.

I lost it to a soldier and a foeman,
    A chap that did not kill me, but he tried;
That took the sabre straight and took it striking
    And laughed and kissed his hand to me and died.

Death in Housman is an instantaneous thing; his heroes don't hang about. 'Shot, so quick, so clean an ending' is the general pattern. And as wars go, the Zulu Wars and the Boer War, which were Housman's wars, were pretty hygienic. Wilfred Owen, who lived and died during Housman's lifetime, told a different sort of truth about war, one which makes it difficult to regard the military element in Housman as little more than a stage setting, a useful prop. When the Great War came, and hundreds of thousands of young men died in battle, it might be thought that Housman would have been particularly affected. In fact, he appears not to have been, and this seems shocking. But poets are not statisticians; to them, one death means more than a thousand. When men are dying like flies, that is what they are dying like.

Still, life has a terrible way of imitating art, and during the war, Housman's college, Trinity, was turned into a hospital, so his daily life came to be peopled by the kind of young men he had written about, but whose endings weren't so quick or so clean. Other dons made them welcome. Housman just complained of the inconvenience. It was all a bit too close to home. The imagination was better, the landscape of the heart more real and more comfortable than the landscape of the trenches.

Tell me not here

(*from* Last Poems)

Tell me not here, it needs not saying,
　　What tune the enchantress plays
In aftermaths of soft September
　　Or under blanching mays,
For she and I were long acquainted
　　And I knew all her ways.

On russet floors, by waters idle,
　　The pine lets fall its cone;
The cuckoo shouts all day at nothing
　　In leafy dells alone;
And traveller's joy beguiles in autumn
　　Hearts that have lost their own.

On acres of the seeded grasses
　　The changing burnish heaves;
Or marshalled under moons of harvest
　　Stand still all night the sheaves;
Or beeches strip in storms for winter
　　And stain the wind with leaves.

Possess, as I possessed a season,
　　The countries I resign,
Where over elmy plains the highway
　　Would mount the hills and shine,
And full of shade the pillared forest
　　Would murmur and be mine.

For nature, heartless, witless nature,
   Will neither care nor know
What stranger's feet may find the meadow
   And trespass there and go,
Nor ask amid the dews of morning
   If they are mine or no.

———————————

Housman's punctiliousness extended to nature as well as to scholarship, and each spring he would note the date that the cherries blossomed in the Cambridge Backs. Some of the trees that blossom there now are trees that Housman saw planted.

Loveliest of trees

(*from* A Shropshire Lad)

Loveliest of trees, the cherry now
Is hung with bloom along the bough,
And stands about the woodland ride
Wearing white for Eastertide.

Now, of my threescore years and ten,
Twenty will not come again,
And take from seventy springs a score,
It only leaves me fifty more.

And since to look at things in bloom
Fifty springs are little room,
About the woodlands I will go
To see the cherry hung with snow.

Cambridge's famous poet could be seen every afternoon taking a walk by one of his regular routes, looking neither to the right nor to the left, and should any acquaintance dare to acknowledge him, they would be steadfastly ignored. At one time, the philosopher Wittgenstein had rooms on the same staircase as Housman lived (as indeed did the art historian and spy Anthony Blunt). Wittgenstein was one day taken short, knocked at Housman's door and asked to use the lavatory. Housman just looked at him, said, 'Certainly not,' and closed the door. It's almost comic, his determination not to be liked.

And yet he enjoyed his celebrity, knowing that heads turned as he passed and saying of his fame that it was like a cushion between him and the hard ground. Of course, his admirers were not expected to approach him. Anyone who took the poems to be messages in code or flags of distress and, on the strength of them, plucked up courage to address what they took to be the real man, the author of *A Shropshire Lad*, found themselves sharply rebuffed. And why not? If he could have revealed the 'real' man, he would hardly have written the poems.

We like to think that artists have a bad time and that this is the price they pay for being able to write their poems and/or their novels. So this seemingly dried-up husk of a man cherishing the memory of a lost love confirms some vague assumptions we have about suffering and art.

I'm not sure this is true. Housman certainly had a better time than his poems let on. He travelled a good deal, went regularly to France – courageously, for that time, by aeroplane – and was rather vain of this daredevil side to his character. He liked tempting fate, and often ran up the several flights of stairs to his room in the hope that he might have a heart attack when he got to the top. Nor was he the ascetic his appearance suggested. Liking good food, he would go on gastronomic tours of France, nosing out in unsuspected corners the remnants of great cellars. And he may have had the occasional fling there, life not quite the sexual Sahara his poems suggest. One should not be surprised if he didn't sometimes grow weary of his thralldom to what was now just a memory. The inner life has its routines and they can be every bit as tedious and irksome as those of the outer life. The grave began to seem a release from love as much as from life.

Crossing alone

(*from* More Poems)

Crossing alone the nighted ferry
    With the one coin for fee,
Whom, on the wharf of Lethe waiting,
    Count you to find? Not me.

The brisk fond lackey to fetch and carry,
    The true, sick-hearted slave,
Expect him not in the just city
    And free land of the grave.

The next poem is Housman at his very best: clear-eyed, un-sentimental, having no truck with God or conventional morality and, in a poem that is full of echoes of the Bible and the Book of Common Prayer, having no patience with either.

Epitaph on an Army of Mercenaries

(*from* Last Poems)

These, in the day when heaven was falling,
  The hour when earth's foundations fled,
Followed their mercenary calling
  And took their wages and are dead.

Their shoulders held the sky suspended;
  They stood, and earth's foundations stay;
What God abandoned, these defended,
  And saved the sum of things for pay.

There are in all of us the remnants of another morality, a persistent rival to Christian and conventional ethics, in which honour, loyalty and pride outweigh modesty and self-denial. It's the morality that prevails in gangster movies and in the western, and the point of Housman's poem is immediately familiar if we set it in the American West and substitute for the mercenaries the reluctant gunslinger and the town lecher. Despised by the respectable (but cowardly) church-going homesteaders, these two social outcasts get together with the drunken doctor and shoot it out with the cattle gang who are holding the town to ransom. It is morality far from its official haunts, an 'Epitaph on an Army of Mercenaries' but also *Gunfight at the O.K. Corral.*

While Housman's poems are autobiographical, his landscapes are the landscapes of the heart. Although the 'blue remembered hills' of the next poem can be identified with the Malverns, they are symbols of a lost time rather than a lost place.

Into my heart an air that kills

(*from* A Shropshire Lad)

Into my heart an air that kills
   From yon far country blows:
What are those blue remembered hills,
   What spires, what farms are those?

That is the land of lost content,
   I see it shining plain,
The happy highways where I went
   And cannot come again.

Once there had been another Housman: good at parody and light verse; even fun, as Lewis Carroll had been fun. Occasionally this surfaces, if rather mordantly, in the poems. In 'Is my team ploughing', Housman has a sour joke at the expense of the departed lover.

Is my team ploughing

(*from* A Shropshire Lad)

'Is my team ploughing,
   That I was used to drive
And hear the harness jingle
   When I was man alive?'

Ay, the horses trample,
   The harness jingles now;
No change though you lie under
   The land you used to plough.

'Is football playing
   Along the river shore,
With lads to chase the leather,
   Now I stand up no more?'

Ay, the ball is flying,
   The lads play heart and soul;
The goal stands up, the keeper
   Stands up to keep the goal.

'Is my girl happy,
   That I thought hard to leave,
And has she tired of weeping
   As she lies down at eve?'

Ay, she lies down lightly,
    She lies not down to weep:
Your girl is well contented.
    Be still, my lad, and sleep.

'Is my friend hearty,
    Now I am thin and pine,
And has he found to sleep in
    A better bed than mine?'

Yes, lad, I lie easy,
    I lie as lads would choose;
I cheer a dead man's sweetheart,
    Never ask me whose.

———————————

If you don't conform in one thing, you must conform in all the others – and Housman had conformed. And yet this drab little man – who still affected the Norfolk jacket and elastic-sided boots and little cap he had worn when he was young – was a pervert, an iconoclast and a blasphemer. Ruthless as an editor, he was pitiless as a critic and contemptuous of all honour and praise. He refused the Order of Merit, and of a colleague who said of him that he was the greatest living Latin scholar, Housman said, 'Well, if I were, he would not know it.' That was one of his voices. But we end with the other.

When summer's end is nighing

(*from* Last Poems)

When summer's end is nighing
　　And skies at evening cloud,
I muse on change and fortune
　　And all the feats I vowed
　　When I was young and proud.

The weathercock at sunset
　　Would lose the slanted ray,
And I would climb the beacon
　　That looked to Wales away
　　And saw the last of day.

From hill and cloud and heaven
　　The hues of evening died;
Night welled through lane and hollow
　　And hushed the countryside,
　　But I had youth and pride.

And I with earth and nightfall
　　In converse high would stand,
Late, till the west was ashen
　　And darkness hard at hand,
　　And the eye lost the land.

The year might age, and cloudy
    The lessening day might close,
But air of other summers
    Breathed from beyond the snows,
    And I had hope of those.

They came and were and are not
    And come no more anew;
And all the years and seasons
    That ever can ensue
    Must now be worse and few.

So here's an end of roaming
    On eves when autumn nighs:
The ear too fondly listens
    For summer's parting sighs,
    And then the heart replies.

———————————

John Betjeman

1906–1984

John Betjeman was born in North London, the only child of affluent parents. He was educated at Marlborough and at Magdalen College, Oxford, where his friends included Auden and MacNeice. He left without taking a degree. At twenty-five, he began writing for the *Architectural Review* and, throughout his life, held passionate views about architecture. Other freelance work included the Shell Guides on Cornwall and Devon and film criticism for the London *Evening Standard* (he later described himself in *Who's Who* as 'a poet and a hack'). His first collection of verse, *Mount Zion*, appeared in 1931, followed by collections including *New Bats in Old Belfries*, *A Few Late Chrysanthemums*, *A Nip in the Air*, *High and Low* and his blank-verse autobiography *Summoned by Bells*. His *Collected Poems* were published in 1958, the first edition selling over 100,000 copies. He was knighted in 1969 and appointed Poet Laureate in 1972. He died in Cornwall in 1984.

Hunter Trials

It's awf'lly bad luck on Diana,
 Her ponies have swallowed their bits;
She fished down their throats with a spanner
 And frightened them all into fits.

So now she's attempting to borrow.
 Do lend her some bits, Mummy, *do*;
I'll lend her my own for to-morrow,
 But to-day *I*'ll be wanting them too.

Just look at Prunella on Guzzle,
 The wizardest pony on earth;
Why doesn't she slacken his muzzle
 And tighten the breech in his girth?

I say, Mummy, there's Mrs Geyser
 And doesn't she look pretty sick?
I bet it's because Mona Lisa
 Was hit on the hock with a brick.

Miss Blewitt says Monica threw it,
 But Monica says it was Joan,
And Joan's very thick with Miss Blewitt,
 So Monica's sulking alone.

And Margaret failed in her paces,
 Her withers got tied in a noose,
So her coronets caught in the traces
 And now all her fetlocks are loose.

Oh, it's me now. I'm terribly nervous.
  I wonder if Smudges will shy.
She's practically certain to swerve as
  Her Pelham is over one eye.

*   *   *   *   *

Oh wasn't it naughty of Smudges?
  Oh, Mummy, I'm sick with disgust.
She threw me in front of the Judges,
  And my silly old collarbone's bust.

———————————————

Writers like to elude their public, lead them a bit of a dance. They take them down untrodden paths, land them in unknown country where they have to ask for directions. Most of the poets in the thirties did that, but not Betjeman. He's always accessible. And, of course, it's a bit of a shock to find that he *is* a thirties poet, just a few months older than Auden, who to his credit was always one of Betjeman's champions. Not that he needed much championing, at any rate in the second part of his life. His verse has an immediate appeal, and as a result he's probably the best-known and the most successful English poet this last century.

It could be said that this was because of television, on which Betjeman was a frequent and indeed an eager performer – but not entirely. Larkin had no truck with television, and when he died the regret and affection for him matched that for Betjeman. Both of them were, of course, very English and wrote straightforward poetry that didn't need much exposition. But it's also the case that poetry, though we don't learn it by heart nowadays and though there is no poetic equivalent of the Booker Prize, still has magic, and seems magical. If their verse chimes in with common experience, poets can still capture the nation's imagination – as, quite apart from his showmanship, Betjeman did.

Much of his verse is backward-looking. As Auden and his friends turned to the proletariat and the future, Betjeman looked back to Victorian and Edwardian models (as, in a different way, did Evelyn Waugh). But why not? Poets don't have to be prophets. The following poem is one of Betjeman's earliest, written in 1930.

Death in Leamington

She died in the upstairs bedroom
  By the light of the ev'ning star
That shone through the plate glass window
  From over Leamington Spa.

Beside her the lonely crochet
  Lay patiently and unstirred,
But the fingers that would have work'd it
  Were dead as the spoken word.

And Nurse came in with the tea-things
  Breast high 'mid stands and chairs –
But Nurse was alone with her own little soul,
  And the things were alone with theirs.

She bolted the big round window,
  She let the blinds unroll,
She set a match to the mantle,
  She covered the fire with coal.

And 'Tea!' she said in a tiny voice
  'Wake up! It's nearly *five*.'
Oh! Chintzy, chintzy cheeriness,
  Half dead and half alive!

Do you know that the stucco is peeling?
  Do you know that the heart will stop?
From those yellow Italianate arches
  Do you hear the plaster drop?

Nurse looked at the silent bedstead,
    At the grey, decaying face,
As the calm of the Leamington ev'ning
    Drifted into the place.

She moved the table of bottles
    Away from the bed to the wall;
And tiptoeing gently over the stairs
    Turned down the gas in the hall.

———————————

Betjeman was born in London at the foot of one of the hills that leads up to Highgate. The charm of this area (which nowadays can be elusive) stayed with him all his life, and his poetry owes as much to childhood as does Wordsworth's. London as it was; England as it was. Anyone fond of architecture in this century has had to watch so much of it destroyed that they condemn themselves to a life of distress and regret, and it is this behind most of Betjeman's poems that gives them a persistent melancholy and sense of loss.

The following poem is about Lissenden Mansions, a block of Edwardian flats opposite Parliament Hill Mansions where Betjeman was born.

N.W.5 and N.6

Red cliffs arise. And up them service lifts
Soar with the groceries to silver heights.
Lissenden Mansions. And my memory sifts
Lilies from lily-like electric lights
And Irish stew smells from the smell of prams
And roar of seas from roar of London trams.

Out of it all my memory carves the quiet
Of that dark privet hedge where pleasures breed,
There first, intent upon its leafy diet,
I watched the looping caterpillar feed
And saw it hanging in a gummy froth
Till, weeks on, from the chrysallis burst the moth.

I see black oak twigs outlined on the sky,
Red squirrels on the Burdett-Coutts estate.
I ask my nurse the question 'Will I die?'
As bells from sad St Anne's ring out so late,
'And if I do die, will I go to Heaven?'
Highgate at eventide. Nineteen-eleven.

'You will. I won't.' From that cheap nursery-maid,
Sadist and puritan as now I see,
I first learned what it was to be afraid,
Forcibly fed when sprawled across her knee
Lock'd into cupboards, left alone all day,
'World without end.' What fearsome words to pray.

'World without end.' It was not what she'd do
That frightened me so much as did her fear
And guilt at endlessness. I caught them too,
Hating to think of sphere succeeding sphere
Into eternity and God's dread will.
I caught her terror then. I have it still.

———————————

Betjeman remembered the cruelties and rebuffs of his child-
hood all too vividly for the rest of his life: that harsh nurse-
maid, a cruel master at his prep school, the tortures of his
first terms at Marlborough. And there were other unbearable
memories. In a Christmas Day broadcast in 1947 he recalled
how his nanny Hannah Wallis, a simple and loving soul, had
bought him a toy for a present, a toy which he wanted and
for which she'd had to save up. In the excitement of unpacking
his stocking he trod on the toy and broke it.

He didn't let on, hiding the debris in his room and saying
nothing to her lest he should hurt her feelings. Later, after
Hannah had tidied his room he found the broken pieces in the
waste-paper basket. Neither of them ever mentioned it. It's a
good job childhood is at the beginning of our lives. We'd
never survive it if it were in the middle.

Now a poem about the Metropolitan Railway. One of
Betjeman's first poems for his school magazine was about
the Metropolitan Railway. It began: 'When travelling to Tim-
buctoo / Don't set out on the Bakerloo.' After Marlborough,
Betjeman went to Oxford, which he left without taking a
degree, and eventually landed up on the staff of the *Arch-
itectural Review* – the *'Archy Rev'* as he called it. Because he
was one of the first champions of Victorian architecture (as
well as of the railway), Betjeman is affectionately regarded
as backward-looking, a fuddy-duddy. In fact, he was a
visionary, detecting quality in the architecture of all periods,
including that most remote of all periods, the recent past.

The Metropolitan Railway

(Baker Street station buffet)

Early Electric! With what radiant hope
   Men formed this many-branched electrolier,
Twisted the flex around the iron rope
   And let the dazzling vacuum globes hang clear,
And then with hearts the rich contrivance fill'd
Of copper, beaten by the Bromsgrove Guild.

Early Electric! Sit you down and see,
   'Mid this fine woodwork and a smell of dinner,
A stained-glass windmill and a pot of tea,
   And sepia views of leafy lanes in PINNER,
Then visualize, far down the shining lines,
Your parents' homestead set in murmuring pines.

Smoothly from HARROW, passing PRESTON ROAD,
   They saw the last green fields and misty sky,
At NEASDEN watched a workmen's train unload,
   And, with the morning villas sliding by,
They felt so sure on their electric trip
That Youth and Progress were in partnership.

And all that day in murky London Wall
   The thought of RUISLIP kept him warm inside;
At FARRINGDON that lunch hour at a stall
   He brought a dozen plants of London Pride;
While she, in arc-lit Oxford Street adrift,
Soared through the sales by safe hydraulic lift.

Early Electric! Maybe even here
    They met that evening at six-fifteen
Beneath the hearts of this electrolier
    And caught the first non-stop to WILLESDEN GREEN,
Then out and on, through rural RAYNERS LANE
To autumn-scented Middlesex again.

Cancer has killed him. Heart is killing her.
    The trees are down. An Odeon flashes fire
Where stood their villa by the murmuring fir
    When 'they would for their children's good conspire.'
Of all their loves and hopes on hurrying feet
Thou art the worn memorial, Baker Street.

———————

In that poem, Betjeman, as always, sees architecture in terms of the people who inhabit it. Churches call up the worshippers, trains the travellers . . . it's always a landscape with figures.

The next poem was written in the fifties, but it ends up with Betjeman remembering, as in so many of his poems, the London he knew as a boy.

Middlesex

Gaily into Ruislip Gardens
    Runs the red electric train,
With a thousand Ta's and Pardon's
    Daintily alights Elaine;
Hurries down the concrete station
With a frown of concentration,
Out into the outskirt's edges
Where a few surviving hedges
Keep alive our lost Elysium – rural Middlesex again.

Well cut Windsmoor flapping lightly,
    Jacqmar scarf of mauve and green
Hiding hair which, Friday nightly,
    Delicately drowns in Drene;
Fair Elaine the bobby-soxer,
Fresh-complexioned with Innoxa,
Gains the garden – father's hobby –
Hangs her Windsmoor in the lobby,
Settles down to sandwich supper and the television screen.

Gentle Brent, I used to know you
    Wandering Wembley-wards at will,
Now what change your waters show you
    In the meadowlands you fill!
Recollect the elm-trees misty
And the footpaths climbing twisty
Under cedar-shaded palings,
Low laburnum-leaned-on railings,
Out of Northolt on and upward to the heights of Harrow hill.

Parish of enormous hayfields
    Perivale stood all alone,
And from Greenford scent of mayfields
    Most enticingly was blown
Over market gardens tidy,
Taverns for the *bona fide*,
Cockney anglers, cockney shooters,
Murray Poshes, Lupin Pooters
Long in Kensal Green and Highgate silent under soot and stone.

Betjeman was quick to cotton on to the power of brand names to evoke a period: 'Well cut Windsmoor', 'Jacqmar scarf'. It's a technique nowadays used by Barry Humphries, of whom Betjeman was an early fan, and by Victoria Wood, and at its best it's a poetry of recognition. The Betjeman family fortunes had actually been based on a brand name. His father was a well-to-do cabinet-maker, and the staple of the firm in Edwardian times was the 'Betjeman Patent Tantalus', a drinks cabinet that could be locked up to defeat the servants.

Betjeman didn't get on with his father, had no intention of following him into the family business, and, quite early, was on the move up the social ladder. This gave him a keen ear for social pretension and the niceties of the language in which it was cloaked, most famously in this poem − a catalogue of snobberies, and apparently a virtual documentary of the expressions used in the Betjeman family home.

How to Get On in Society

Phone for the fish-knives, Norman
    As Cook is a little unnerved;
You kiddies have crumpled the serviettes
    And I must have things daintily served.

Are the requisites all in the toilet?
    The frills round the cutlets can wait
Till the girl has replenished the cruets
    And switched on the logs in the grate.

It's ever so close in the lounge, dear,
    But the vestibule's comfy for tea
And Howard is out riding on horseback
    So do come and take some with me.

Now here is a fork for your pastries
    And do use the couch for your feet;
I know what I wanted to ask you –
    Is trifle sufficient for sweet?

Milk and then just as it comes dear?
    I'm afraid the preserve's full of stones;
Beg pardon, I'm soiling the doileys
    With afternoon tea-cakes and scones.

A social climber himself, Betjeman always had a keen and kindly eye for those on the lower slopes.

Business Girls

From the geyser ventilators
    Autumn winds are blowing down
On a thousand business women
    Having baths in Camden Town.

Waste pipes chuckle into runnels,
    Steam's escaping here and there,
Morning trains through Camden cutting
    Shake the Crescent and the Square.

Early nip of changeful autumn,
    Dahlias glimpsed through garden doors,
At the back precarious bathrooms
    Jutting out from upper floors;

And behind their frail partitions
    Business women lie and soak,
Seeing through the draughty skylight
    Flying clouds and railway smoke.

Rest you there, poor unbelov'd ones,
    Lap your loneliness in heat.
All too soon the tiny breakfast,
    Trolley-bus and windy street!

The operative line in that poem is 'Rest you there, poor unbelov'd ones'. Betjeman always had an eye for the forlorn and the unloved: unloved buildings, unloved suburbs, aesthetic outcasts as well as emotional ones. Lord David Cecil was once giving a lecture on 'The Pleasures of Reading' when, rather to his surprise, he saw Betjeman in the audience. Afterwards he thanked him for coming. 'Oh no, don't thank me,' said Betjeman. 'I thought it was the pleasures of Reading.' Reading, I suppose, yet another unloved place.

This love of the neglected came from thinking himself a bit unloved, which of course he wasn't, certainly not when he was older. And from this came all the business of carrying his teddy bear about with him, which, I have to say, I find a bit tiresome. Mind you, writers often pretend they suffer more than they do, or blame other people for the suffering they cause themselves. One should never underestimate the extent to which writers steal. They burgle other people's lives, and one of the things they most commonly purloin is other people's pain.

In his long poem *Summoned by Bells*, Betjeman describes the horrors suffered by new boys at Marlborough, but they don't seem actually to have happened to him. Indeed, he seems to have played the system very well. Louis MacNeice, who was at the same school, described the boy Betjeman (and the phrase describes his life) as 'a triumphant misfit'. He got along in life by playing up as 'Silly Me' so that people were always rallying round. The Silly Mes of this world often get their own way and can be bullies, and so it was occasionally with Betjeman. None of this matters unless you're on the receiving end, and as long as the writer keeps coming up with the goods.

Betjeman, unlike many of his contemporaries, wasn't homosexual, but he did make a tentative stab at conforming in this regard. Indeed, on one occasion, he said to Hugh Gaitskell, 'Do you mind if I put my hand on your bottom?' The future leader of the Labour Party sighed and said, 'Well, if you *must.*'

Betjeman's 'type' seems to have been brisk and masterful like the hearty girls he celebrated in his poems, and he married the daughter of the Commander-in-Chief of the Army in India, Field Marshal Chetwode. His father-in-law was a bit of a tartar, though in no time at all Betjeman had him eating out of his hand, the Field Marshal even tucking rugs over the poet's knees. Field Marshal Chetwode was not unlike one of the old men 'who never cheated, never doubted' mentioned in the next poem.

Death of King George V

'NEW KING ARRIVES IN HIS CAPITAL BY AIR . . .'
Daily Newspaper

Spirits of well-shot woodcock, partridge, snipe
    Flutter and bear him up the Norfolk sky:
In that red house in a red mahogany book-case
    The stamp collection waits with mounts long dry.

The big blue eyes are shut which saw wrong clothing
    And favourite fields and coverts from a horse;
Old men in country houses have clocks ticking
    Over thick carpets with a deadened force;

Old men who never cheated, never doubted,
    Communicated monthly, sit and stare
At the new suburb stretched beyond the run-way
    Where a young man lands hatless from the air.

In his later years, Betjeman tended to become public property. He was a natural television performer, audiences loving his 'gosh and golly' approach. His personality had always been something of a turn, though, and now an act perfected for a small audience was simply transferred to the electronic stage.

However, his clowning should never make us forget that he had a marvellous ear for language. It's the limited language of the middle class, or of those aspiring to be so, but he was a master of it.

Devonshire Street, W.1

The heavy mahogany door with its wrought-iron screen
   Shuts. And the sound is rich, sympathetic, discreet.
The sun still shines on this eighteenth-century scene
   With Edwardian faience adornments – Devonshire Street.

No hope. And the X-ray photographs under his arm
   Confirm the message. His wife stands timidly by.
The opposite brick-built house looks lofty and calm
   Its chimneys steady against a mackerel sky.

No hope. And the iron knob of this palisade
   So cold to the touch, is luckier now than he.
'Oh merciless, hurrying Londoners! Why was I made
   For the long and painful deathbed coming to me?'

She puts her fingers in his as, loving and silly,
   At long-past Kensington dances she used to do
'It's cheaper to take the tube to Piccadilly
   And then we can catch a nineteen or a twenty-two.'

It's almost impertinent to comment on a poem like this, it's so limpid and clear. But what makes it unbearable is the little snatch of ordinary speech at the finish. Although it's the man who is going to die, it's the woman we see most clearly and who is the pathetic figure.

Even in a little cameo like the next poem, it is Betjeman's language – and one characteristic word – that brings the scene into focus.

In a Bath Teashop

'Let us not speak, for the love we bear one another –
        Let us hold hands and look.'
She, such a very ordinary little woman;
        He, such a thumping crook;
But both, for a moment, little lower than the angels
        In the teashop's ingle-nook.

'Thumping' is what does it. There is so much of Betjeman in the word.

'The proof of a poet', said Walt Whitman, 'is that his country absorbs him as affectionately as he has absorbed it.' Betjeman was so English it was almost a joke and, with his popularity as a performer as well as a poet, his country certainly absorbed him. But he survived his celebrity because he was tough, and he was tough because, despite his terrible raincoats and battered pork-pie hats, he was a dandy and dandies are tough. The times have only just caught up with his taste and proved him as much of a prophet as Auden – 'triumphant misfit' is right.

There are absences. An artist can be diminished by his virtues and one of Betjeman's virtues is clarity. However much the reader welcomes clarity, some of the most memorable moments in poetry occur when it isn't exactly clear what the poet is talking about. Auden has many such moments, but Betjeman never, because he always is sure, and that's the penalty of being lucid. He may be pretending it's light verse when it isn't, but he knows exactly what he's about. His is not poetry of ideas or argument, but because it is simple doesn't mean that there's nothing to understand.

And he always hits home.

---

from Five O'Clock Shadow

A haze of thunder hangs on the hospital rose-beds,
    A doctors' foursome out on the links is played,
Safe in her sitting-room Sister is putting her feet up:
    This is the time of day when we feel betrayed.

Below the windows, loads of loving relations
    Rev in the car park, changing gear at the bend,
Making for home and a nice big tea and the telly:
    'Well, we've done what we can. It can't be long till the end.'

W. H. Auden

1907–1973

Wystan Hugh Auden was born in York, brought up in Birmingham, where his father was a physician, and educated at Gresham's School, Holt, and Christ Church, Oxford. His student contemporaries included poets Cecil Day Lewis, Louis MacNeice and Stephen Spender. After graduating in 1929, he spent several months in Berlin, often in the company of Christopher Isherwood, his future collaborator. His first book, *Poems*, was published in 1930 by T. S. Eliot at Faber and Faber and he later become associated with Rupert Doone's Group Theatre, for which he wrote several plays, sometimes in collaboration with Isherwood. In January 1939 the two of them left England for the United States, where Auden became a citizen in 1946. His later works include *The Age of Anxiety, Nones, The Shield of Achilles* and *Homage to Clio*, and he also wrote texts for works by Benjamin Britten and (with Chester Kallman) the libretto for Stravinsky's opera *The Rake's Progress*. Elected Professor of Poetry at Oxford in 1956, he died in Vienna in 1973.

On This Island

Look, stranger, on this island now
The leaping light for your delight discovers,
Stand stable here
And silent be,
That through the channels of the ear
May wander like a river
The swaying sound of the sea.

Here at a small field's ending pause
Where the chalk wall falls to the foam and its tall ledges
Oppose the pluck
And knock of the tide,
And the shingle scrambles after the suck-
-ing surf, and a gull lodges
A moment on its sheer side.

Far off like floating seeds the ships
Diverge on urgent voluntary errands,
And this full view
Indeed may enter
And move in memory as now these clouds do,
That pass the harbour mirror
And all the summer through the water saunter.

Much of Auden, even most of Auden, and even some of that first little snatch of Auden, I do not understand. Now, I could say the same for Ezra Pound or Eliot's *The Waste Land*, but there the difficulty is plain: you know you don't understand Pound or T. S. Eliot right from the start. Auden is different. It seems easy. The landscape's familiar, there are no out-of-the-way references, and as often as not there's a gripping opening line to get you off to a good start – only it doesn't last.

I'm not saying that the poems begin well, then taper off, though they do begin well. Auden has some wonderful opening lines:

> August for the people and their favourite islands . . .

> What siren zooming is sounding our coming . . .

> Out on the lawn I lie in bed,
> Vega conspicuous overhead . . .

And of course, perhaps his most famous lines:

> Lay your sleeping head, my love,
> Human on my faithless arm . . .

But once he's got you with one of these lines, and certainly in his early poems, he's off into a territory of his own, an alternative world of leaders, gangs, frontiers and flight, on what Seamus Heaney has called 'those oddly unparaphrasable riffs'.

'He gets carried away' would be another way of putting it, though Christopher Isherwood, with whom he often collaborated in the thirties, said that the obscurity could also be put down to the fact that Auden was very lazy:

> He hated polishing and making corrections. If he didn't like a poem, he threw it away and wrote another. If I liked one line, he would keep it and work it into a new poem. In this way, whole poems were constructed which were simply anthologies of my favourite lines, entirely regardless of grammar or sense.

'This', said Isherwood, 'is the simple explanation of much of Auden's celebrated obscurity.' More writers have worked like that, Shakespeare included, than is generally admitted, and at least it puts literary criticism in its place.

Some poems don't require exposition, though. Auden was fascinated by verse in all its forms, and this is a pastiche of an eighteenth-century ballad, transformed into a nightmare:

O What Is That Sound

O what is that sound which so thrills the ear
   Down in the valley drumming, drumming?
Only the scarlet soldiers, dear,
   The soldiers coming.

O what is that light I see flashing so clear
   Over the distance brightly, brightly?
Only the sun on their weapons, dear,
   As they step lightly.

O what are they doing with all that gear,
   What are they doing this morning, this morning?
Only their usual manoeuvres, dear,
   Or perhaps a warning.

O why have they left the road down there,
   Why are they suddenly wheeling, wheeling?
Perhaps a change in their orders, dear.
   Why are you kneeling?

O haven't they stopped for the doctor's care,
   Haven't they reined their horses, their horses?
Why, they are none of them wounded, dear,
   None of these forces.

O is it the parson they want, with white hair,
   Is it the parson, is it, is it?
No, they are passing his gateway, dear,
   Without a visit.

O it must be the farmer who lives so near.
  It must be the farmer so cunning, so cunning?
They have passed the farmyard already, dear,
  And now they are running.

O where are you going? Stay with me here!
  Were the vows you swore deceiving, deceiving?
No, I promised to love you, dear,
  But I must be leaving.

O it's broken the lock and splintered the door,
  O it's the gate where they're turning, turning;
Their boots are heavy on the floor
  And their eyes are burning.

———————————

Auden is good at casting a spell, hinting at horrors just around the corner, and he uses Hitchcock's technique of investing the ordinary and domestic with nightmare and suspense. Some of it manages to be prophetic. If Auden is a great poet, this ability to prophesy is one constituent of his greatness.

from The Witnesses

I shouldn't dance.
We're afraid in that case you'll have a fall;
We've been watching you over the garden wall
  For hours
The sky is darkening like a stain;
Something is going to fall like rain,
  And it won't be flowers.

Nobody in the thirties was quite sure what war would be like, whether there would be gas, for instance, or aerial bombardment. There's a stock and rather a silly question: 'Why was there no poetry written in the Second World War?' One answer is that there was, but it was written in the ten years before the war started.

Auden was a landscape poet, though of a rather particular kind. The son of a doctor, he was born in York in 1907 but brought up in Solihull in the heart of the industrial Midlands. Not the landscape of conventional poetic inspiration but, for Auden, magical:

from Letter to Lord Byron

But let me say before it has to go,
  It's the most lovely country that I know;
Clearer than Scafell Pike, my heart has stamped on
The view from Birmingham to Wolverhampton.

Long, long ago, when I was only four,
  Going towards my grandmother, the line
Passed through a coal-field. From the corridor
  I watched it pass with envy, thought 'How fine!
  Oh how I wish that situation mine.'
Tramlines and slagheaps, pieces of machinery,
That was, and still is, my ideal scenery.

At Oxford, he was already writing and publishing poetry. To his contemporaries, he was a magnetic figure, partly because he seemed to have all the answers, a characteristic that his later self came to deplore, though he remained a bit of an intellectual bully all his life. As a man, he was insecure and unhappy and doesn't seem to have fallen in love until he went to America in 1939, but this didn't stop him prescribing for the love affairs of his friends.

The Danish philosopher Kierkegaard says that there are two ways: one is to suffer; the other is to become a professor of the fact that another suffers. Auden was to play both roles in his time; but when he was an undergraduate, he was undoubtedly a professor.

Who's Who

A shilling life will give you all the facts:
How Father beat him, how he ran away,
What were the struggles of his youth, what acts
Made him the greatest figure of his day:
Of how he fought, fished, hunted, worked all night,
Though giddy, climbed new mountains; named a sea:
Some of the last researchers even write
Love made him weep his pints like you and me.

With all his honours on, he sighed for one
Who, say astonished critics, lived at home;
Did little jobs about the house with skill
And nothing else; could whistle; would sit still
Or potter round the garden; answered some
Of his long marvellous letters but kept none.

Auden taught at various prep schools in the early thirties, and one of the criticisms that contemporaries made of his poetry was that his view of the world was dictated by his unhappy experiences at school. 'The best reason I have for opposing Fascism', he said, 'is that at school I lived in a Fascist state.' Not a statement that would commend itself to someone actually having to live in a Fascist state, and the kind of remark that made him blush once he got away from England in 1939. 'All the verse I wrote,' Auden said later,

> all the positions I took in the thirties didn't save a single Jew. These writings, these attitudes only help oneself. They merely make people who think like one admire and like one, which is rather embarrassing.

Which is true, but which says nothing about the poetry, and embarrassing though the older Auden found his younger self, the poetry of that younger self survives the embarrassment.

The turning point in Auden's life came, or is supposed to have come, when he and Isherwood went to the United States at the start of 1939 and stayed there, both eventually becoming American citizens. Silly people at the time took this to be cowardice, which it wasn't, and even people who admired him thought Auden's poetry was never as good afterwards. But this wasn't true either.

Why Auden left England has been much discussed. Auden liked feeling at home, but he didn't like feeling at home where he felt at home. England was too cosy. He would never grow up there, he thought. He would always be the *enfant terrible*, the prisoner of his public and court poet to the Left. At least this is how Auden came to see it.

But it wasn't quite like that either. All that had happened was that he had gone to America in 1939, seemingly with no plans to stay, and, for the first time in his life, he had fallen in love – with Chester Kallman, with whom he was to live happily and unhappily for the rest of his life. It just happened that change in private places went with change in public places, love and war coinciding: Auden really was just an early 'GI bride'. Somebody who cared more about what people thought would have come back when war started, but Auden – and it was one of the winning characteristics in a personality that was not always attractive – didn't care tuppence what people thought.

As it turned out, going to America turned out to be a deliverance, the kind of escape an established writer often craves, a way of eluding his public, of not having to go on writing in the same way, of not having to imitate himself. 'By the time you have perfected a style of writing', said George Orwell, 'you have always outgrown it.' 'You spend twenty-five years learning to be yourself,' said Auden, 'and then you find you must now start learning not to be yourself' – and it took him a while. This next poem Auden called a 'hangover from home'. He wrote it in America, but one of the reasons he left England, he said, was to stop writing poetry like this.

September 1, 1939

I sit in one of the dives
On Fifty-second Street
Uncertain and afraid
As the clever hopes expire
Of a low dishonest decade:
Waves of anger and fear
Circulate over the bright
And darkened lands of the earth,
Obsessing our private lives;
The unmentionable odour of death
Offends the September night.

Accurate scholarship can
Unearth the whole offence
From Luther until now
That has driven a culture mad,
Find what occurred at Linz,
What huge imago made
A psychopathic god:
I and the public know
What all schoolchildren learn,
Those to whom evil is done
Do evil in return.

Exiled Thucydides knew
All that a speech can say
About Democracy,
And what dictators do,
The elderly rubbish they talk
To an apathetic grave;
Analysed in his book,
The enlightenment driven away,
The habit-forming pain,
Mismanagement and grief:
We must suffer them all again.

Into this neutral air
Where blind skyscrapers use
Their full height to proclaim
The strength of Collective Man,
Each language pours its vain
Competitive excuse:
But who can live for long
In an euphoric dream;
Out of the mirror they stare,
Imperialism's face
And the international wrong.

Faces along the bar
Cling to their average day:
The lights must never go out,
The music must always play,
All the conventions conspire
To make this fort assume
The furniture of home;
Lest we should see where we are,
Lost in a haunted wood,
Children afraid of the night
Who have never been happy or good.

The windiest militant trash
Important Persons shout
Is not so crude as our wish:
What mad Nijinsky wrote
About Diaghilev
Is true of the normal heart;
For the error bred in the bone
Of each woman and each man
Craves what it cannot have,
Not universal love
But to be loved alone.

From the conservative dark
Into the ethical life
The dense commuters come,
Repeating their morning vow;
'I will be true to the wife,
I'll concentrate more on my work,'
And helpless governors wake
To resume their compulsory game:
Who can release them now,
Who can reach the deaf,
Who can speak for the dumb?

All I have is a voice
To undo the folded lie,
The romantic lie in the brain
Of the sensual man-in-the-street
And the lie of Authority
Whose buildings grope the sky:
There is no such thing as the State
And no one exists alone;
Hunger allows no choice
To the citizen or the police;
We must love one another or die.

Defenceless under the night
Our world in stupor lies:
Yet, dotted everywhere,
Ironic points of light
Flash out wherever the Just
Exchange their messages:
May I, composed like them
Of Eros and of dust,
Beleaguered by the same
Negation and despair,
Show an affirming flame.

———————————

In America, Auden's poetry began to take on a different tone. His 'old grand manner', as he described it, proceeded from 'a resonant heart'. With the war and the Cold War that followed:

from We Too Had Known Golden Hours

All words like Peace and Love,
All sane affirmative speech,
Had been soiled, profaned, debased
To a horrid mechanical screech.

And so the tone of his poetry grew more wry and ironic and, as he got older, increasingly intimate and domestic.

Not that his circumstances were ever conventionally cosy; he and Kallman lived in some squalor. They weren't home-makers, either of them, though Kallman was a good cook. The Stravinskys came round to supper one night. Madame Stravinsky – endearingly named Vera – was paying a call of nature when she spotted a bowl of dirty water on the bath-room floor. In a forlorn attempt to give the place a woman's touch, she emptied the contents down the wash-basin, only to discover later that this was to have been the *pièce de résistance* of the meal: a chocolate pudding. The basin was, incidentally, the same in which Auden routinely pissed. Where, one wonders, did one wash one's hands after one had washed one's hands?

The next poem was written in 1948.

A Walk After Dark

A cloudless night like this
Can set the spirit soaring:
After a tiring day
The clockwork spectacle is
Impressive in a slightly boring
Eighteenth-century way.

It soothed adolescence a lot
To meet so shameless a stare;
The things I did could not
Be so shocking as they said
If that would still be there
After the shocked were dead.

Now, unready to die
But already at the stage
When one starts to resent the young,
I am glad those points in the sky
May also be counted among
The creatures of middle-age.

It's cosier thinking of night
As more an Old People's Home
Than a shed for a faultless machine,
That the red pre-Cambrian light
Is gone like Imperial Rome
Or myself at seventeen.

Yet however much we may like
The stoic manner in which
The classical authors wrote,
Only the young and the rich
Have the nerve or the figure to strike
The lacrimae rerum note

For the present stalks abroad
Like the past and its wronged again
Whimper and are ignored,
And the truth cannot be hid;
Somebody chose their pain,
What needn't have happened did.

Occurring this very night
By no established rule,
Some event may already have hurled
Its first little No at the right
Of the laws we accept to school
Our post-diluvian world:

But the stars burn on overhead,
Unconscious of final ends,
As I walk home to bed,
Asking what judgement waits
My person, all my friends,
And these United States.

———————————

The apartment in which Auden and Kallman lived was in a rather seedy area on the Lower East Side and had formerly belonged to an abortionist, which resulted in frequent misunderstandings. On one occasion, a young woman from Hunter College knocked at the door. Auden answered, and after beating about the bush for some time, she eventually plucked up the courage to say, 'But aren't you an abortionist?' 'No,' said Auden flatly. 'Poet.'

The story has a point in that there was a matter-of-factness in his approach to writing, and although he didn't actually put 'poet' on a brass plate on the door, he did feel that a poet should be able to turn his hand to anything in verse – to wedding poems, poems for celebrations, librettos, poems in obscure metres – and he took great pride in being a craftsman able to produce these to order. This, though, is one of his earlier and best-known poems, written in 1938:

Musée des Beaux Arts

About suffering they were never wrong,
The Old Masters: how well they understood
Its human position; how it takes place
While someone else is eating or opening a window or just
    walking dully along;
How, when the aged are reverently, passionately waiting
For the miraculous birth, there always must be
Children who did not specially want it to happen, skating
On a pond at the edge of the wood:
They never forgot
That even the dreadful martyrdom must run its course
Anyhow in a corner, some untidy spot
Where the dogs go on with their doggy life and the
    torturer's horse
Scratches its innocent behind on a tree.

In Brueghel's *Icarus*, for instance: how everything turns away
Quite leisurely from the disaster; the ploughman may
Have heard the splash, the forsaken cry,
But for him it was not an important failure; the sun shone
As it had to on the white legs disappearing into the green
Water; and the expensive delicate ship that must have seen
Something amazing, a boy falling out of the sky,
Had somewhere to get to and sailed calmly on.

Auden thought of poetry as dual: poetry as song, poetry as truth. It's perhaps this that, in his poem 'Their Lonely Betters', written in 1950, made him sceptical of birds who sing without feeling and with no regard for truth.

Their Lonely Betters

As I listened from a beach-chair in the shade
To all the noises that my garden made,
It seemed to me only proper that words
Should be withheld from vegetables and birds.

A robin with no Christian name ran through
The Robin-Anthem which was all it knew,
And rustling flowers for some third party waited
To say which pairs, if any, should get mated.

Not one of them was capable of lying,
There was not one which knew that it was dying
Or could have with a rhythm or a rhyme
Assumed responsibility for time.

Let them leave language to their lonely betters
Who count some days and long for certain letters;
We, too, make noises when we laugh or weep:
Words are for those with promises to keep.

Auden died in Vienna in 1973, when he was only sixty-six, but it would be hard to say his work was not finished. His output had been prodigious, and he went on working right until the end in a routine that was every bit as rigid as that of Housman, whom he so briskly diagnosed when he was a young man ('Deliberately he chose the dry-as-dust, / Kept tears like dirty postcards in a drawer'). But you're no more likely to find consistency in a writer than you would in a normal human being. Besides, as Auden himself said: 'At thirty I tried to vex my elders. Past sixty it's the young whom I hope to bother.'

I would be hard put to say what a great poet is, but part of it, in Auden's case, is the obscurity with which I started. If his life has to be divided into two parts, there are great poems in both. Perhaps he was too clever for the English. Bossy and not entirely likeable, when he died his death occasioned less regret than that of Larkin or Betjeman, though he was the greater poet. This would not have concerned him as he was not vain: criticism seldom bothered him nor did he covet praise or money. And though he would have quite liked the Nobel Prize, all he demanded at the finish was punctuality.

I'll end with the final part of the poem Auden wrote in memory of another poet, W. B. Yeats, who died in January 1939. The last two lines are inscribed on Auden's memorial in Westminster Abbey.

from In Memory of W. B. Yeats

(d. Jan. 1939)

Earth, receive an honoured guest:
William Yeats is laid to rest.
Let the Irish vessel lie
Emptied of its poetry.

Time that is intolerant
Of the brave and innocent,
And indifferent in a week
To a beautiful physique,

Worships language and forgives
Everyone by whom it lives;
Pardons cowardice, conceit,
Lays its honours at their feet.

Time that with this strange excuse
Pardoned Kipling and his views,
And will pardon Paul Claudel,
Pardons him for writing well.

In the nightmare of the dark
All the dogs of Europe bark,
And the living nations wait,
Each sequestered in its hate;

Intellectual disgrace
Stares from every human face,
And the seas of pity lie
Locked and frozen in each eye.

Follow, poet, follow right
To the bottom of the night,
With your unconstraining voice
Still persuade us to rejoice;

With the farming of a verse
Make a vineyard of the curse,
Sing of human unsuccess
In a rapture of distress;

In the deserts of the heart
Let the healing fountain start,
In the prison of his days
Teach the free man how to praise.

———————————

Louis MacNeice

1907–1963

L ouis MacNeice was born in Belfast the son of a bookish Church of Ireland minister, a bishop-to-be. Academically precocious, he was already writing verse at seven, around the time of his mother's death. He was educated in England at Sherborne and Marlborough. At Merton College, Oxford, he made the acquaintance of Auden and Spender and published his first book of poems, *Blind Fireworks* (1929). He worked subsequently as a translator, literary critic, playwright, autobiographer, BBC producer and feature writer. In 1941 he was appointed scriptwriter/producer in BBC Radio's Features Department, where he worked until his death. *Letters from Iceland* (1937) was written in collaboration with Auden. Subsequent collections include *The Earth Compels, Autumn Journal, Plant and Phantom, Springboard, Holes in the Sky* and *Autumn Sequel*. MacNeice published highly acclaimed translations including the *Agamemnon* of Aeschylus (1936) and Goethe's *Faust*. He scripted more than 150 radio plays, including *The Dark Tower* (1947). *The Burning Perch*, his last volume of poems, appeared shortly before his death in 1963.

Prayer before Birth

I am not yet born; O hear me.
Let not the bloodsucking bat or the rat or the stoat or the
   club-footed ghoul come near me.

I am not yet born, console me.
I fear that the human race may with tall walls wall me,
   with strong drugs dope me, with wise lies lure me,
      on black racks rack me, in blood-baths roll me.

I am not yet born; provide me
With water to dandle me, grass to grow for me, trees to talk
   to me, sky to sing to me, birds and a white light
      at the back of my mind to guide me.

I am not yet born; forgive me
For the sins that in me the world shall commit, my words
   when they speak me, my thoughts when they think me,
      my treason engendered by traitors beyond me,
         my life when they murder by means of my
            hands, my death when they live me.

I am not yet born; rehearse me
In the parts I must play and the cues I must take when
   old men lecture me, bureaucrats hector me, mountains
      frown at me, lovers laugh at me, the white
         waves call me to folly and the desert calls
            me to doom and the beggar refuses
               my gift and my children curse me.

I am not yet born; O hear me,
Let not the man who is beast or who thinks he is God
   come near me.

I am not yet born; O fill me
With strength against those who would freeze my
   humanity, would dragoon me into a lethal automaton,
      would make me a cog in a machine, a thing with
         one face, a thing, and against all those
            who would dissipate my entirety, would
               blow me like thistledown hither and
                  thither or hither and thither
                     like water held in the
                        hands would spill me.

Let them not make me a stone and let them not spill me.
Otherwise kill me.

———————————

The public like labels (or newspapers think they do), and particularly when it comes to art and literature, which are both potentially dangerous or at least awkward to handle. 'The Poets of the Thirties', which is itself a label, generally comes in a nice boxed set labelled 'Auden and Co.' – that is, W. H. Auden, Stephen Spender, Cecil Day Lewis and Louis MacNeice.

This must have been more irritating for Spender, Day Lewis and Co. than it was for Auden, though it's true they all knew one another, had been at the same schools or known one another at university, and sometimes collaborated. But then came the war and they went their different ways, some of them not seeming to survive the loss of their corporate identity, just as actors who have been a big hit when with the National Theatre or the Royal Shakespeare Company then go off on their own and are lost sight of. One should never underestimate the importance of one's *setting*. When Louis MacNeice died in 1963, an obituary (admittedly in a Chicago newspaper) identified him as 'a writer with the BBC' and concluded: 'He was formerly a poet.'

Carrickfergus

I was born in Belfast between the mountain and the gantries
    To the hooting of lost sirens and the clang of trams:
Thence to Smoky Carrick in County Antrim
    Where the bottle-neck harbour collects the mud which jams

The little boats beneath the Norman castle,
    The pier shining with lumps of crystal salt;
The Scotch Quarter was a line of residential houses
    But the Irish Quarter was a slum for the blind and halt.

The brook ran yellow from the factory stinking of chlorine,
    The yarn-mill called its funeral cry at noon;
Our lights looked over the lough to the lights of Bangor
    Under the peacock aura of a drowning moon.

The Norman walled this town against the country
    To stop his ears to the yelping of his slave
And built a church in the form of a cross but denoting
    The list of Christ on the cross in the angle of the nave.

I was the rector's son, born to the anglican order,
    Banned for ever from the candles of the Irish poor;
The Chichesters knelt in marble at the end of a transept
    With ruffs about their necks, their portion sure.

The war came and a huge camp of soldiers
    Grew from the ground in sight of our house with long
Dummies hanging from gibbets for bayonet practice
    And the sentry's challenge echoing all day long;

A Yorkshire terrier ran in and out by the gate-lodge
  Barred to civilians, yapping as if taking affront:
Marching at ease and singing 'Who Killed Cock Robin?'
  The troops went out by the lodge and off to the Front.

The steamer was camouflaged that took me to England –
  Sweat and khaki in the Carlisle train;
I thought that the war would last for ever and sugar
  Be always rationed and that never again

Would the weekly papers not have photos of sandbags
  And my governess not make bandages from moss
And the people not have maps above the fireplace
  With flags on pins moving across and across –

Across the hawthorn hedge the noise of bugles,
  Flares across the night,
Somewhere on the lough was a prison ship for Germans,
  A cage across their sight.

I went to school in Dorset, the world of parents
  Contracted into a puppet world of sons
Far from the mill girls, the smell of porter, the salt-mines
  And the soldiers with their guns.

———————————

The concerns of writers are selfish and to be born in Northern Ireland is to inherit a set of circumstances which, however painful, are also useful: they are something to write out of. It was less so in MacNeice's youth, and though, as a child, he was shocked by the poverty of the Carrickfergus Catholics, he seldom dealt explicitly with his divided country. His concerns were generally more personal. His father was a Church of Ireland rector, an Anglican who later became a bishop, and MacNeice's childhood seems to have bred in him a melancholy and an aloofness that always set him apart.

Stephen Spender tells a story how, when the Soviet Union came into the war in 1941, the British ambassador Sir Archibald Clark-Kerr thought he would give a party for British poets with a view to putting them in touch with their Soviet counterparts.

Throughout this party, MacNeice – sleek, dark and expressionless – leaned against the chimney-piece, glass in hand, looking infinitely removed from his colleagues. At the end of the evening, Clark-Kerr went up to him and said, 'Is it true you were brought up in Belfast at Carrickfergus?'

MacNeice said, 'Yes, it is.'

'Ah,' said Clark-Kerr, 'then that confirms a legend I have heard: that, centuries ago, a race of seals invaded that coast and interbred with the population. Good night.'

The following is a sad poem about the death of MacNeice's mother when he was five.

Autobiography

In my childhood trees were green
And there was plenty to be seen.

Come back early or never come.

My father made the walls resound,
He wore his collar the wrong way round.

Come back early or never come.

My mother wore a yellow dress;
Gently, gently, gentleness.

Come back early or never come.

When I was five the black dreams came;
Nothing after was quite the same.

Come back early or never come.

The dark was talking to the dead;
The lamp was dark beside my bed.

Come back early or never come.

When I woke they did not care;
Nobody, nobody was there.

Come back early or never come.

When my silent terror cried,
Nobody, nobody replied.

Come back early or never come.

I got up; the chilly sun
Saw me walk away alone.

Come back early or never come.

———————————————

When MacNeice did walk away, it was to school in England, to Marlborough, where he was rather hearty, though not wholeheartedly so. MacNeice was never very good at being wholehearted. His closest friend at school was not hearty at all but the very aesthetic Anthony Blunt. At Oxford, it was much the same. MacNeice wrote poetry but didn't quite fit in. 'Homosexuality and intelligence, heterosexuality and brawn were almost inexorably paired. This left me out,' he said, 'and I took to drink.' And though most of the other poets and literary figures either took a poor degree or left early with no degree at all, MacNeice – a 'natural examinee and intellectual window-dresser' as he described himself – took a double first. One catches already the note – it's a very English note – of someone who can do it but deprecates the doing of it, a nice characteristic in a man but not always much help to a writer.

So while Auden and Isherwood were whooping it up in Berlin, MacNeice went off to Birmingham as a lecturer in classics. And that was the way it was going to be, too. MacNeice always on the edge of the group . . . a radical but never a Marxist, a bohemian but fond of family life.

'I would have a poet,' he said,

> able bodied, fond of talking, a reader of the newspapers, capable of pity and laughter, informed in economics, appreciative of women, involved in personal relation- ships, actively interested in politics,

susceptible to physical impressions . . . I write poems not because it is smart to be a poet but because I enjoy it as one enjoys swimming or swearing, and also because it is my road to freedom and knowledge.

This is the poet as good chap.

Apart from his empirical attitude towards politics, the other thing that set MacNeice apart from many of his contemporaries was that he loved women.

from Trilogy for X

(*first part*)

When clerks and navvies fondle
  Beside canals their wenches,
In rapture or in coma
  The haunches that they handle,
And the orange moon sits idle
  Above the orchard slanted –
Upon such easy evenings
  We take our loves for granted.

But when, as now, the creaking
  Trees on the hills of London
Like bison charge their neighbours
  In wind that keeps us waking
And in the draught the scalloped
  Lampshade swings a shadow,
We think of love bound over –
  The mortgage on the meadow.

And one lies lonely, haunted
  By limbs he half remembers,
And one, in wedlock, wonders
  Where is the girl he wanted;
And some sit smoking, flicking
  The ash away and feeling
For love gone up like vapour
  Between the floor and ceiling.

But now when winds are curling
    The trees do you come closer,
Close as an eyelid fasten
    My body in darkness, darling;
Switch the light off and let me
    Gather you up and gather
The power of trains advancing
    Further, advancing further.

———————————

There's something of Auden in that poem. Auden was never very good on women but he was very good on canals, which he had practically privatised along with pylons and factories and all the other paraphernalia of what MacNeice called 'the placid dotage of a great industrial country'. It's a pity neither of them is around today.

Anybody writing poetry in the thirties had somehow to come to terms with Auden; MacNeice's 'Trilogy for X', in praise of women, was a way of doing that. Auden, you see, had got a head start on the other poets. He'd got into the thirties first, like someone taking over the digs. He'd rampaged through all the rooms, sprawled in every chair, slept in every bed, put his books on the bookshelves, scattered his stuff all over the dressing table and left the bathroom in a disgusting state, all the time singing at the top of his voice. When the other poets began to arrive, they spent a lot of their time trying to find a place they could call their own, somewhere safe from Auden, where they could hear the sound of their own voices. When Auden finally went off to America at the end of the decade, they must have heaved a sigh of relief. From their point of view, it was perhaps a pity that he hadn't gone five years earlier.

MacNeice lived much of his life in Primrose Hill in London, hard by the zoo, and he wrote a book about zoos:

The pleasure of dappled things, the beauty of adaptation to purpose, the glory of extravagance, classic elegance or romantic nonsense and grotesquerie – all these we get from the Zoo. We react to these with the same delight as to new potatoes in April speckled with chopped parsley or to the lights at night on the Thames at Battersea Power House, or to cars sweeping their shadows from lamp-post to lamp-post down Haverstock Hill or to brewer's drays or to lighthouses and searchlights or to a newly cut lawn or to a hot towel or a friction at the barber's or to Moran's two classic tries at Twickenham in 1937 or to the smell of dusting-powder in a warm bathroom or to the fun of shelling peas into a china bowl or of shuffling one's feet through dead leaves when they are crisp or to the noise of rain or the crackling of a newly lit fire or the jokes of a street-hawker or the silence of snow in moonlight or the purring of a powerful car.

from *Zoo* (1938)

This isn't a man who's frightened of being thought ordinary, and it's this and his refusal to sink his individuality in some Marxist generality – 'become part of the pattern in the lino', as he put it – that got MacNeice labelled 'bourgeois', even by some of his friends. Of course, he had that very English fault: an overdose of irony. Irony stops you being wholehearted, stops you going overboard. But, of course, if you don't go overboard, you tend not to make a splash, and it's this, rather than anything lacking in his poems, that makes MacNeice the least known of the poets of his generation. Here's another personal poem, about marriage.

Les Sylphides

Life in a day: he took his girl to the ballet;
Being shortsighted himself could hardly see it –
    The white skirts in the grey
    Glade and the swell of the music
    Lifting the white sails.

Calyx upon calyx, canterbury bells in the breeze
The flowers on the left mirror to the flowers on the right
    And the naked arms above
    The powdered faces moving
    Like seaweed in a pool.

Now, he thought, we are floating – ageless, oarless –
Now there is no separation, from now on
    You will be wearing white
    Satin and a red sash
    Under the waltzing trees.

But the music stopped, the dancers took their curtain,
The river had come to a lock – a shuffle of programmes –
    And we cannot continue down
    Stream unless we are ready
    To enter the lock and drop.

So they were married – to be the more together –
And found they were never again so much together,
    Divided by the morning tea,
    By the evening paper,
    By children and tradesmen's bills.

Waking at times in the night she found assurance
Due to his regular breathing but wondered whether
    It was really worth it and where
    The river had flowed away
    And where were the white flowers.

———————————

That MacNeice turned out to have been right in hedging his bets during the thirties didn't help his reputation either. His longest poem, *Autumn Journal,* is a personal record of the period from August to December 1938, the months that include Munich and the triumph of Franco's forces in Barcelona. MacNeice writes as he always wrote as a private man, these public events jumbled together in his mind with the private ones: the breakup of his marriage and his sense of futility.

He liked fast cars (which was another way of getting away from Auden), and in this extract from *Autumn Journal* he drives up to Oxford to take part in a by-election in which the Left and the disaffected Right joined forces to support A. D. Lindsay, the Master of Balliol, in an unsuccessful attempt to defeat the Appeasement candidate, Quentin Hogg, later Lord Hailsham.

from Autumn Journal

The next day I drove by night
    Among red and amber and green, spears and candles,
Corkscrews and slivers of reflected light
    In the mirror of the rainy asphalt
Along the North Circular and the Great West roads
    Running the gauntlet of impoverished fancy
Where housewives bolster up their jerry-built abodes
    With *amour propre* and the habit of Hire Purchase.
The wheels whished in the wet, the flashy strings
    Of neon lights unravelled, the windscreen-wiper
Kept at its job like a tiger in a cage or a cricket that sings
    All night through for nothing.
Factory, a site for a factory, rubbish dumps,
    Bungalows in lath and plaster, in brick, in concrete,
And shining semi-circles of petrol pumps
    Like intransigent gangs of idols.
And the road swings round my head like a lassoo
    Looping wider and wider tracts of darkness
And the country succeeds the town and the country too
    Is damp and dark and evil.
And coming over the Chilterns the dead leaves leap
    Charging the windscreen like a barrage of angry
Birds as I take the steep
    Plunge to Henley or Hades.
And at the curves of the roads the telephone wires
    Shine like strands of silk and the hedge solicits
My irresponsible tyres
    To an accident, to a bed in the wet grasses.

And in quiet crooked streets only the village pub
    Spills a golden puddle
Over the pavement and trees bend down and rub
    Unopened dormer windows with their knuckles.
Nettlebed, Shillingford, Dorchester – each unrolls
    The road to Oxford; *Qu'allais-je faire* to-morrow
Driving voters to the polls
    In that home of lost illusions?
And what am I doing it for?
    Mainly for fun, partly for a half-believed-in
Principle, a core
    Of fact in a pulp of verbiage,
Remembering that this crude and so-called obsolete
    Top-heavy tedious parliamentary system
Is our only ready weapon to defeat
    The legions' eagles and the lictors' axes;
And remembering that those who by their habit hate
    Politics can no longer keep their private
Values unless they open the public gate
    To a better political system.
That Rome was not built in a day is no excuse
    For *laissez-faire*, for bowing to the odds against us;
What is the use
    Of asking what is the use of one brick only?
The perfectionist stands for ever in a fog
    Waiting for the fog to clear; better to be vulgar
And use your legs and leave a blank for Hogg
    And put a cross for Lindsay.
There are only too many who say 'What difference does it make

One way or the other?
To turn the stream of history will take
    More than a by-election.'
So Thursday came and Oxford went to the polls
    And made its coward vote and the streets resounded
To the triumphant cheers of the lost souls –
    The profiteers, the dunderheads, the smarties.
And I drove back to London in the dark of the morning, the trees
    Standing out in the headlights cut from cardboard;
Wondering which disease
    Is worse – the Status Quo or the Mere Utopia.
For from now on
    Each occasion must be used, however trivial,
To rally the ranks of those whose chance will soon be gone
    For even guerrilla warfare.
The nicest people in England have always been the least
    Apt to solidarity or alignment
But all of them must now align against the beast
    That prowls at every door and barks in every headline.
Dawn and London and daylight and last the sun:
    I stop the car and take the yellow placard
Off the bonnet; that little job is done
    Though without success or glory.
The plane-tree leaves come sidling down
    (Catch my guineas, catch my guineas)
And the sun caresses Camden Town,
    The barrows of oranges and apples.

———————

What is appealing about MacNeice is that he wasn't a man for certainties. He couldn't wholeheartedly support either side, and his poetry is about being in two minds – that is, the state most of us are in most of the time.

After the war, MacNeice's reputation dwindled. He had begun working for the BBC in 1941, and though he produced some memorable broadcasts, this didn't improve his reputation as a poet. Nor did it improve his poetry, and it wasn't until the late fifties that he hit his stride again and began to write as well as, and better than, he'd done in the thirties. But he didn't have much time left.

MacNeice died quite young, in 1963, having caught pneumonia down a pothole in Yorkshire while recording authentic sound effects for one of his BBC programmes. There was a memorial service at the BBC church – All Souls, Langham Place – where Auden (one is tempted to say 'of course') gave the address. He praised MacNeice's poetry and also praised his character, saying that he sponged on no one, cheated no one, provided for his family and paid his bills. It was MacNeice the decent chap. These were virtues Auden himself had come to rather late in life, the virtues of the good citizen rather than the good poet, for whom they're really not virtues at all, doing the right thing not always the right thing to do. He also praised MacNeice, saying he had been the first to appreciate good work by his contemporaries. However, that can work both ways, too; sometimes you need the envy and the jealousy to get the engine going.

One feels quite safe saying these things about MacNeice, knowing full well that this ironic, melancholic and disdainful man would have been the first they would have occurred to. He was a man riven by doubt and duality and made a virtue out of it, and his poems are full of debate. The others might make fools of themselves over Communism or boys or religion or tinpot psychology, but he didn't make a fool of himself. He wasn't single-minded enough . . . but perhaps not to be single-minded, that was to be the real fool. E. M. Forster said of himself that he had been nibbled away by kindness, lust and fun – they had diminished him. And in this respect, the common sense that makes him so sympathetic diminished MacNeice. Perhaps he recognised this:

The Slow Starter

A watched clock never moves, they said:
Leave it alone and you'll grow up.
Nor will the sulking holiday train
Start sooner if you stamp your feet.
   He left the clock to go its way;
   The whistle blew, the train went gay.

Do not press me so, she said;
Leave me alone and I will write
But not just yet, I am sure you know
The problem. Do not count the days.
   He left the calendar alone;
   The postman knocked, no letter came.

O never force the pace, they said;
Leave it alone, you have lots of time,
Your kind of work is none the worse
For slow maturing. Do not rush.
   He took their tip, he took his time,
   And found his time and talent gone.

Oh you have had your chance, It said;
Left it alone and it was one.
Who said a watched clock never moves?
Look at it now. Your chance was I.
   He turned and saw the accusing clock
   Race like a torrent round a rock.

Leaving it like that, it's a sad story, but it has a happy ending. MacNeice has now been dead long enough to be ripe for re-discovery. I'm not sure that's quite a happy ending, involving as it does articles in the Sunday supplements beginning 'Shares in MacNeice are rising . . .': something Larkin was perhaps predicting as early as 1963 when he wrote of MacNeice's 'poetry of everyday life, of shop windows, traffic policemen, ice cream sodas, lawn mowers and an uneasy awareness of what the newsboys were shouting'.

'And then,' one feels Larkin is thinking, 'then comes *me!*'

There is, though, appreciation much closer to home – that is, MacNeice's home. Some of the liveliest and most accomplished poetry being written today comes from Northern Ireland. The English may think of MacNeice as an Auden sidekick, and in Dublin he's still an outsider, but with the younger poets of Northern Ireland – Derek Mahon and Paul Muldoon – MacNeice comes into his own; they have picked up frequencies in his work inaudible in Dublin and London but not in Belfast. Never a poet of Northern Ireland (*'Come back early or never come'*), MacNeice has nevertheless bequeathed to its poets in their shameful time a perspective and a detachment, a concern for the private in the confusion of the public that he learned in another shameful time.

I almost end with a poem that might be thought to be about ecology, though I think it's about the imagination.

To Posterity

When books have all seized up like the books in graveyards
And reading and even speaking have been replaced
By other, less difficult, media, we wonder if you
Will find in flowers and fruit the same colour and taste
They held for us for whom they were framed in words,
And will your grass be green, your sky be blue,
Or will your birds be always wingless birds?

But finally a lovely, touching poem, one of the best Mac-Neice ever wrote and which deserves a place in every anthology of twentieth-century poetry.

Death of an Actress

I see from the paper that Florrie Forde is dead –
Collapsed after singing to wounded soldiers,
At the age of sixty-five. The American notice
Says no doubt all that need be said

About this one-time chorus girl; whose rôle
For more than forty stifling years was giving
Sexual, sentimental, or comic entertainment,
A gaudy posy for the popular soul.

Plush and cigars: she waddled into the lights,
Old and huge and painted, in velvet and tiara,
Her voice gone but around her head an aura
Of all her vanilla-sweet forgotten vaudeville nights.

With an elephantine shimmy and a sugared wink
She threw a trellis of Dorothy Perkins roses
Around an audience come from slum and suburb
And weary of the tea-leaves in the sink;

Who found her songs a rainbow leading west
To the home they never had, to the chocolate Sunday
Of boy and girl, to cowslip time, to the never-
Ending weekend Islands of the Blest.

In the Isle of Man before the war before
The present one she made a ragtime favourite
Of 'Tipperary', which became the swan-song
Of troop-ships on a darkened shore;

And during Munich sang her ancient quiz
Of *Where's Bill Bailey?* and the chorus answered,
Muddling through and glad to have no answer:
Where's Bill Bailey? How do *we* know where he is!

Now on a late and bandaged April day
In a military hospital Miss Florrie
Forde has made her positively last appearance
And taken her bow and gone correctly away.

Correctly. For she stood
For an older England, for children toddling
Hand in hand while the day was bright. Let the wren
    and robin
Gently with leaves cover the Babes in the Wood.

Philip Larkin

1922–1985

Philip Larkin was born in Coventry. He was educated at King Henry VIII School, Coventry, and St John's College, Oxford, where he was a contemporary of Kingsley Amis. 1945 saw the publication of his first book of poetry, *North Ship*, followed by two novels, *Jill* (1946) and *A Girl in Winter* (1947). Subsequent collections include *The Less Deceived* (1955), *The Whitsun Weddings* (1964) and *High Windows* (1974). He wrote two books of journalism, *All What Jazz: A Record Library* and *Required Writing: Miscellaneous Prose*, and edited the *Oxford Book of Twentieth Century English Verse*. For twelve years he worked in campus libraries before taking charge of the Hull University library from 1955 until his death. He was the recipient of innumerable honours, including the Queen's Gold Medal for Poetry. One critic said that Larkin was 'a laureate too obvious to need official recognition'. He died in 1985.

I Remember, I Remember

Coming up England by a different line
For once, early in the cold new year,
We stopped, and, watching men with number-plates
Sprint down the platform to familiar gates,
'Why, Coventry!' I exclaimed. 'I was born here.'

I leant far out, and squinnied for a sign
That this was still the town that had been 'mine'
So long, but found I wasn't even clear
Which side was which. From where those cycle-crates
Were standing, had we annually departed

For all those family hols? . . . A whistle went:
Things moved. I sat back, staring at my boots.
'Was that,' my friend smiled, 'where you "have your roots"?'
No, only where my childhood was unspent,
I wanted to retort, just where I started:

By now I've got the whole place clearly charted.
Our garden, first: where I did not invent
Blinding theologies of flowers and fruits,
And wasn't spoken to by an old hat.
And here we have that splendid family

I never ran to when I got depressed,
The boys all biceps and the girls all chest,
Their comic Ford, their farm where I could be
'Really myself'. I'll show you, come to that,
The bracken where I never trembling sat,

Determined to go through with it; where she
Lay back, and 'all became a burning mist'.
And, in those offices, my doggerel
Was not set up in blunt ten-point, nor read
By a distinguished cousin of the mayor,

Who didn't call and tell my father *There
Before us, had we the gift to see ahead* –
'You look as if you wished the place in Hell,'
My friend said, 'judging from your face.' 'Oh well,
I suppose it's not the place's fault,' I said.

'Nothing, like something, happens anywhere.'

———————————

Larkin is famous for his fear of death. He's also famous for his fear of life. When I first read Larkin, it wasn't the fear of extinction that rang a bell; I was still young enough to think that bells like that only tolled for other people. It was recognition of a different sort, familiarity not so much with the feelings he was talking about as with the places. And the sense that, most of the time to most people, nothing much happens. Life is elsewhere. There were the provinces for a start, where nothing ever happened; libraries, where I'd spent half my life; churches, where I'd spent the other. Until I read Larkin – and in particular 'I Remember, I Remember' – I'd never imagined such experiences, or non-experiences, could be the stuff of poetry, still less the credentials for writing, or that anybody could write, not about the something but the nothing that happens anywhere.

When he first started writing poetry, before he learned the sound of his own voice, Larkin wrote like Auden. Then, when he got to university, it was Yeats. Finally, he discovered Hardy, whom he liked, he said, because he taught him that he didn't have to 'jack himself up' into poetry. It could be ordinary and about ordinary things, which suited him.

His childhood he characterised as 'a forgotten boredom'. His father was the city treasurer of Coventry and they don't seem to have got on.

This Be The Verse

They fuck you up, your mum and dad.
  They may not mean to, but they do.
They fill you with the faults they had
  And add some extra, just for you.

But they were fucked up in their turn
  By fools in old-style hats and coats,
Who half the time were soppy-stern,
  And half at one another's throats.

Man hands on misery to man
  It deepens like a coastal shelf.
Get out as early as you can,
  And don't have any kids yourself.

This poem seems to show that Larkin didn't get on with his parents but, as he said in an interview, he did get on with them; it was just that they weren't very good at being happy. The poem, which certainly doesn't jack itself up, echoes a short one of Hardy's.

> I'm Smith of Stoke, aged sixty-odd,
> I've lived without a dame
> From youth-time on; and would to God
> My dad had done the same.

Even if Larkin hadn't got on with his parents, I still think he was wrong to complain about it. If your parents do fuck you up and you're going to write, that's fine because then you've got something to write about. But if they don't fuck you up, then you've got nothing to write about, so then they've fucked you up good and proper.

The problem arises in the first instance because we think of novels as something made up but poems as messages from the heart. Larkin must be telling the truth about himself because that's what poems do – just as, in Housman's case, his poems were flags of distress, an SOS from the soul. But a poet can counterfeit. He can put on a personality and impersonate just as a novelist can. And the 'I' that writes is never quite the same as the 'I' written. Kingsley Amis, who knew Larkin well, says that some of Larkin's poems were by the man he knew, but others were by someone else entirely. The 'I' is always the eye. It is not always *I*.

This next poem was possibly occasioned by the marriage of an ex-girlfriend; it's certainly very different from the last one.

Maiden Name

Marrying left your maiden name disused.
Its five light sounds no longer mean your face,
Your voice, and all your variants of grace;
For since you were so thankfully confused
By law with someone else, you cannot be
Semantically the same as that young beauty:
It was of her that these two words were used.

Now it's a phrase applicable to no one,
Lying just where you left it, scattered through
Old lists, old programmes, a school prize or two,
Packets of letters tied with tartan ribbon –
Then is it scentless, weightless, strengthless, wholly
Untruthful? Try whispering it slowly.
No, it means you. Or, since you're past and gone,

It means what we feel now about you then:
How beautiful you were, and near, and young,
So vivid, you might still be there among
Those first few days, unfingermarked again.
So your old name shelters our faithfulness,
Instead of losing shape and meaning less
With your depreciating luggage laden.

Larkin went to Oxford at the start of the war, then became a librarian, working in various places before landing up at Hull University, where he remained for the rest of his life as librarian of the Brynmor Jones Library. The library had been endowed by Sir Brynmor Jones, who once came there on a visit. Meeting him in the library, Larkin said, was like being in St Pancras Station and coming across St Pancras.

The library was to Larkin as textual criticism was to Housman: something at which he excelled but which made no demands on his other life. But he cared about it.

> New eyes each year
> Find old books here,
> And new books, too,
> Old eyes renew;
> So youth and age
> Like ink and page
> In this house join,
> Minting new coin.

This next poem is about a return visit to Oxford, and in the background, as so often in Larkin (and Hardy), is the railway.

Dockery and Son

'Dockery was junior to you,
Wasn't he?' said the Dean. 'His son's here now.'
Death-suited, visitant, I nod. 'And do
You keep in touch with –' Or remember how
Black-gowned, unbreakfasted, and still half-tight
We used to stand before that desk, to give
'Our version' of 'these incidents last night'?
I try the door of where I used to live:

Locked. The lawn spreads dazzlingly wide.
A known bell chimes. I catch my train, ignored.
Canal and clouds and colleges subside
Slowly from view. But Dockery, good Lord,
Anyone up today must have been born
In '43, when I was twenty-one.
If he was younger, did he get this son
At nineteen, twenty? Was he that withdrawn

High-collared public-schoolboy, sharing rooms
With Cartwright who was killed? Well, it just shows
How much . . . How little . . . Yawning, I suppose
I fell asleep, waking at the fumes
And furnace-glares of Sheffield, where I changed,
And ate an awful pie, and walked along
The platform to its end to see the ranged
Joining and parting lines reflect a strong

Unhindered moon. To have no son, no wife,
No house or land still seemed quite natural.
Only a numbness registered the shock
Of finding out how much had gone of life,
How widely from the others. Dockery, now:
Only nineteen, he must have taken stock
Of what he wanted, and been capable
Of . . . No, that's not the difference: rather, how

Convinced he was he should be added to!
Why did he think adding meant increase?
To me it was dilution. Where do these
Innate assumptions come from? Not from what
We think truest, or most want to do:
Those warp tight-shut, like doors. They're more a style
Our lives bring with them: habit for a while,
Suddenly they harden into all we've got

And how we got it; looked back on, they rear
Like sand-clouds, thick and close, embodying
For Dockery a son, for me nothing,
Nothing with all a son's harsh patronage.
Life is first boredom, then fear.
Whether or not we use it, it goes,
And leaves what something hidden from us chose,
And age, and then the only end of age.

I don't, alas, know much about the technicalities of poetry. Like most people, I recognise a thumping metre and an obvious rhyme and not much more. But poetry isn't just prose that's been through the shredder, and it's only after reading Larkin's poems a few times that one senses how well they're constructed, the rhymes lurking just under the surface so that what seems casual and even discursive is actually carefully structured. Larkin's remark about MacNeice – 'He always brings the kite down safely' – applies equally well to Larkin himself.

Larkin generally feels, or affects to feel, shut out, though the language he uses in order to say so signals that he still wants to be recognised as a member of the human race, and a pretty straightforward one at that. He has one poem which begins:

> When I see a couple of kids
> And guess he's fucking her and she's
> Taking the pill or wearing a diaphragm,
> I know this is paradise

> Everyone old has dreamed of all their lives –
> Bonds and gestures pushed to one side
> Like an outdated combine harvester,
> And everyone young going down the long slide

> To happiness, endlessly . . .

Well. Not quite. Yes, one wants to say, but . . . Of course, Larkin wrote that in 1967, a few months before this:

Annus Mirabilis

Sexual intercourse began
In nineteen sixty-three
(Which was rather late for me) –
Between the end of the *Chatterley* ban
And the Beatles' first LP.

Up till then there'd only been
A sort of bargaining,
A wrangle for a ring,
A shame that started at sixteen
And spread to everything.

Then all at once the quarrel sank:
Everyone felt the same,
And every life became
A brilliant breaking of the bank,
A quite unlosable game.

So life was never better than
In nineteen sixty-three
(Though just too late for me) –
Between the end of the *Chatterley* ban
And the Beatles' first LP.

Larkin didn't want to be thought nice, and sometimes wasn't. A friend of mine – the writer Neville Smith – was a student at Hull and found himself at a bus stop with Larkin. It was pouring with rain and Larkin had an umbrella. Neville edged closer and closer to the poet until finally Larkin said, 'Don't think you're coming under my umbrella.'

'Don't think you're coming under my umbrella' could serve as a description of a number of his poems. The temptation of all art is to console, but Larkin's poems seldom attempt to.

This next poem would, I suppose, nowadays be called a 'green' poem, though properly construed, all poems are green. It was written in 1971, when its sentiments were rather less modish than they are today.

Going, Going

I thought it would last my time –
The sense that, beyond the town,
There would always be fields and farms,
Where the village louts could climb
Such trees as were not cut down;
I knew there'd be false alarms

In the papers about old streets
And split-level shopping, but some
Have always been left so far;
And when the old part retreats
As the bleak high-risers come
We can always escape in the car.

Things are tougher than we are, just
As earth will always respond
However we mess it about;
Chuck filth in the sea, if you must:
The tides will be clean beyond.
– But what do I feel now? Doubt?

Or age, simply? The crowd
Is young in the M1 café;
Their kids are screaming for more –
More houses, more parking allowed,
More caravan sites, more pay.
On the Business Page, a score

Of spectacled grins approve
Some takeover bid that entails
Five per cent profit (and ten
Per cent more in the estuaries): move
Your works to the unspoilt dales
(Grey area grants)! And when

You try to get near the sea
In summer . . .
                    It seems, just now,
To be happening so very fast;
Despite all the land left free
For the first time I feel somehow
That it isn't going to last,

That before I snuff it, the whole
Boiling will be bricked in
Except for the tourist parts –
First slum of Europe: a role
It won't be so hard to win,
With a cast of crooks and tarts.

And that will be England gone,
The shadows, the meadows, the lanes,
The guildhalls, the carved choirs.
There'll be books; it will linger on
In galleries; but all that remains
For us will be concrete and tyres.

Most things are never meant.
This won't be, most likely: but greeds
And garbage are too thick-strewn
To be swept up now, or invent
Excuses that make them all needs.
I just think it will happen, soon.

———————————

That poem was written for the Department of the Environment. What Larkin didn't foresee was that one of the things that was going was the ability of government departments to spend money on poems.

Now a poem called '1914', though the title is written in Roman numerals, as if it were carved on a war memorial.

MCMXIV

Those long uneven lines
Standing as patiently
As if they were stretched outside
The Oval or Villa Park,
The crowns of hats, the sun
On moustached archaic faces
Grinning as if it were all
An August Bank Holiday lark;

And the shut shops, the bleached
Established names on the sunblinds,
The farthings and sovereigns,
And dark-clothed children at play
Called after kings and queens,
The tin advertisements
For cocoa and twist, and the pubs
Wide open all day;

And the countryside not caring:
The place-names all hazed over
With flowering grasses, and fields
Shadowing Domesday lines
Under wheat's restless silence;
The differently-dressed servants
With tiny rooms in huge houses,
The dust behind limousines;

Never such innocence,
Never before or since,
As changed itself to past
Without a word – the men
Leaving the gardens tidy,
The thousands of marriages
Lasting a little while longer:
Never such innocence again.

————————————

If poetry is the highest form of writing, it's because it does so much with so little. That poem, only thirty-two lines, says as much as a play or a film.

In 1954, Larkin wrote a poem about work, in which he pictured it as a toad: 'Why should I let the toad work / Squat on my life?' This poem, written nearly ten years later, takes a mellower view, with Larkin now rather easier on himself.

Toads Revisited

Walking around in the park
Should feel better than work:
The lake, the sunshine,
The grass to lie on,

Blurred playground noises
Beyond black-stockinged nurses –
Not a bad place to be.
Yet it doesn't suit me,

Being one of the men
You meet of an afternoon:
Palsied old step-takers,
Hare-eyed clerks with the jitters,

Waxed-fleshed out-patients
Still vague from accidents,
And characters in long coats
Deep in the litter-baskets –

All dodging the toad work
By being stupid or weak.
Think of being them!
Hearing the hours chime,

Watching the bread delivered,
The sun by clouds covered,
The children going home;
Think of being them,

Turning over their failures
By some bed of lobelias,
Nowhere to go but indoors,
No friends but empty chairs –

No, give me my in-tray,
My loaf-haired secretary,
My shall-I-keep-the-call-in-Sir:
What else can I answer,

When the lights come on at four
At the end of another year?
Give me your arm, old toad;
Help me down Cemetery Road.

———————

Larkin relished dullness. 'Deprivation is for me', he said famously, 'what daffodils are for Wordsworth.' But he also said that however negative some of his poems might seem, one should never forget that writing a poem was never negative; to write a poem is a very positive thing to do.

This poem was inspired by a tomb in Chichester Cathedral, and it's among Larkin's best known and most hopeful.

An Arundel Tomb

Side by side, their faces blurred,
The earl and countess lie in stone,
Their proper habits vaguely shown
As jointed armour, stiffened pleat,
And that faint hint of the absurd –
The little dogs under their feet.

Such plainness of the pre-baroque
Hardly involves the eye, until
It meets his left-hand gauntlet, still
Clasped empty in the other; and
One sees, with a sharp tender shock,
His hand withdrawn, holding her hand.

They would not think to lie so long.
Such faithfulness in effigy
Was just a detail friends would see:
A sculptor's sweet commissioned grace
Thrown off in helping to prolong
The Latin names around the base.

They would not guess how early in
Their supine stationary voyage
The air would change to soundless damage,
Turn the old tenantry away;
How soon succeeding eyes begin
To look, not read. Rigidly they

Persisted, linked, through lengths and breadths
Of time. Snow fell, undated. Light
Each summer thronged the glass. A bright
Litter of birdcalls strewed the same
Bone-riddled ground. And up the paths
The endless altered people came,

Washing at their identity.
Now, helpless in the hollow of
An unarmorial age, a trough
Of smoke in slow suspended skeins
Above their scrap of history,
Only an attitude remains:

Time has transfigured them into
Untruth. The stone fidelity
They hardly meant has come to be
Their final blazon, and to prove
Our almost-instinct almost true:
What will survive of us is love.

Larkin's last long poem 'Aubade' was printed in the *Times Literary Supplement* in 1977. I remember it being something of an event: you asked friends if they'd seen it. It was what it must have been like in the nineteenth century when poetry was news.

By this time, though, Larkin was writing less and less. He hadn't abandoned poetry, he said; poetry had abandoned him. In *The Ballad of Reading Gaol*, Wilde says that he who lives more lives than one, more deaths than one must die, and not being able to write was a kind of death, though one which Larkin bore stoically and with his usual grim humour, comparing it to going bald – nothing he could do about it. But he did regret it very much, and it made the last years of his life all the bleaker.

Aubade

I work all day, and get half-drunk at night.
Waking at four to soundless dark, I stare.
In time the curtain-edges will grow light.
Till then I see what's really always there:
Unresting death, a whole day nearer now,
Making all thought impossible but how
And where and when I shall myself die.
And interrogation: yet the dread
Of dying, and being dead,
Flashes afresh to hold and horrify.

The mind blanks at the glare. Not in remorse
– The good not done, the love not given, time
Torn off unused – nor wretchedly because
An only life can take so long to climb
Clear of its wrong beginnings, and may never;
But at the total emptiness for ever,
The sure extinction that we travel to
And shall be lost in always. Not to be here,
Not to be anywhere,
And soon; nothing more terrible, nothing more true.

This is a special way of being afraid
No trick dispels. Religion used to try,
That vast moth-eaten musical brocade
Created to pretend we never die,
And specious stuff that says *No rational being
Can fear a thing it will not feel*, not seeing

That this is what we fear – no sight, no sound,
No touch or taste or smell, nothing to think with,
Nothing to love or link with,
The anaesthetic from which none come round.

And so it stays just on the edge of vision,
A small unfocused blur, a standing chill
That slows each impulse down to indecision.
Most things may never happen: this one will,
And realisation of it rages out
In furnace-fear when we are caught without
People or drink. Courage is no good:
It means not scaring others. Being brave
Lets no one off the grave.
Death is no different whined at than withstood.

Slowly light strengthens, and the room takes shape.
It stands plain as a wardrobe, what we know,
Have always known, know that we can't escape,
Yet can't accept. One side will have to go.
Meanwhile telephones crouch, getting ready to ring
In locked-up offices, and all the uncaring
Intricate rented world begins to rouse.
The sky is white as clay, with no sun.
Work has to be done.
Postmen like doctors go from house to house.

When Larkin died, there was a great and unexpected out-pouring of public affection and appreciation, some of which, though, he must have been aware of during his lifetime. He had always tried to dodge the public, letting his second nature – the grim pessimism of so many of his poems – do duty for the whole man. 'I have a great shrinking from pub-licity,' he wrote to the novelist Barbara Pym. 'Think of me as A. E. Housman without the talent or the scholarship. Or the curious private life.'

Still, when one is dead, one's life is no longer one's own, and though his diaries were burned, biographical and critical studies now loom, and what we feel now about Larkin then is perhaps another reason why he regarded death with such a marked lack of enthusiasm. If anything, after his death there was too much glad endorsement of the bleaker side of his verse, a lot of jumping on his bandwagon (if a hearse can be a bandwagon), so I'd like to finish on a more optimistic note. I ended the Hardy section with a poem – 'Proud Songsters' – that was almost cheerful, and with Larkin's admiration for and debt to Hardy, it's appropriate to end this one with a poem very like it in spirit.

The Trees

The trees are coming into leaf
Like something almost being said;
The recent buds relax and spread,
Their greenness is a kind of grief.

Is it that they are born again
And we grow old? No, they die too.
Their yearly trick of looking new
Is written down in rings of grain.

Yet still the unresting castles thresh
In fullgrown thickness every May.

Last year is dead, they seem to say,
Begin afresh, afresh, afresh.

Index of Titles and First Lines

Acknowledgements

The publishers gratefully acknowledge permission to reprint copyright material in this book as follows:

Poems by John Betjeman taken from *Collected Poems* (John Murray, 2006) © John Betjeman by permission of The Estate of John Betjeman

Poems by W. H. Auden taken from *Collected Poems*, edited by Edward Mendelson (Faber and Faber Ltd, 2007) © The Estate of W. H. Auden. Reprinted by permission of Curtis Brown, Ltd

Poems by Louis MacNeice © Louis MacNeice, taken from *Collected Poems*, edited by Peter McDonald (Faber and Faber Ltd, 2007) by permission of David Higham Associates, London

Poems by Philip Larkin taken from *The Complete Poems* edited by Archie Burnett (Faber and Faber Ltd, 2012) © The Estate of Philip Larkin

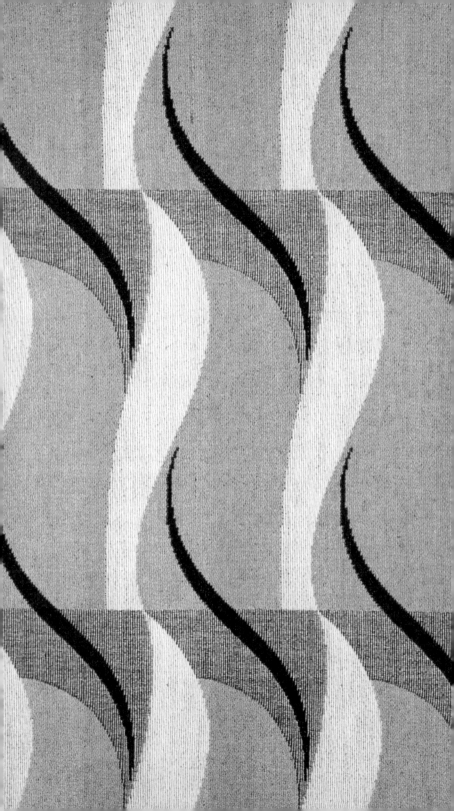